The Art of 'Ware

Bruce Webster

M&T BOOKS

First Edition—1995

Printed in the United States of America.

10 9 8 7 6 5 4 3 2 1

```
Webster, Bruce F.
     The art of 'ware : Sun Tzu's classic work reinterpreted /
        by Bruce F. Webster.
       p. cm.
     Includes index.
     ISBN: 1-55851-396-5
     1. Sun-tzu, --6th cent. B.C. -- Sun-tzu ping fa.
     2. New Products.  3. Marketing.  4. Industrial management.
     5. Success in business  I. Title
     HF5415.153 .W43        1995
     658 20                                      95025004
                                                 CIP
```

Trademarks

Associate Publisher: Paul Farrell
Managing Editor: Cary Sullivan
Copy Edit Manager: Shari Chappell
Editor: Debra Williams Cauley
Production Editor: Joseph McPartland
Copy Editor: Annette Devlin
Development Editor: Ezra Shapiro

*To Drinda
with love forever*

Contents

Acknowledgments

First, let me thank Sun Tzu for having written a stunning piece of work some 2,500 years ago; I also must thank those who have preserved it through the years and those who have translated it in modern times. If there is any brilliance in this book, it comes from Sun Tzu; I am merely along for the ride.

I must also acknowledge all that I have learned from the various opportunities given me over the past twenty years, especially from the people I've worked with. Special credit goes to my five years at Pages Software Inc as a member of Team Banzai. The experience of going from two engineers in a cheap office to a full-blown company with several million dollars in venture funding was exhausting, exhilarating, and educational; watching the same company succumb to market forces was likewise an exhausting education.

Much credit for this book must go to Carole McClendon of the Waterside Agency for pitching the idea to various publishers; to Brenda McLaughlin and Steve Berkowitz for accepting that idea; and to Debra Williams Cauley at M&T Books for helping turn my manuscript into the book you're holding.

Significant thanks go to Ezra Shapiro, who didn't let a long friendship get in the way of being honest about changes and improvements that the manuscript needed. Eric Nee, editor-in-chief of *Upside*, generously took time to read and critique an early draft. At ARINC, Mitch Baxter gave feedback on the almost-final draft, while Bill Stewart became the first person to cite The *Art of 'Ware* in a company memo dictating a particular course of action. The combined input of these and other friends made the book much better than it would have been otherwise.

My wonderful wife Sandra, as always, provided unflagging encouragement, support, and love, while our children, home and abroad,—Chase, Aaron, Jacqui, Heather, Bethan, Wesley, Jon, Crystal, and Emily—provided enthusiasm when my own was lagging.

All responsibility for the contents of this book is mine.

Bruce F. Webster
San Diego, California   August, 1995

Introduction

It is a cliché to say that we live in times of turmoil and upheaval, but that makes it no less true. Our national and global economies are undergoing a sea change into something which we do not, I think, fully understand, and the process is neither easily managed nor soon ended. At the forefront are the technology-driven markets: computer hardware, software, telecommunications, biotechnology, information, and entertainment—the so-called convergence industries. Technology churn causes these industries and companies to reinvent themselves every two to five years. The pace seems to be picking up, not slowing down, driven by the commercial emergence of the first new information utility in half a century: the Internet, with its public face, the World Wide Web. And through this all, the distance from the leading edge of technology back to its trailing edge is ever shrinking.

Too many good ideas, good products, good technologies die or waste away because the companies involved—especially the small start-ups—don't know how to carve out and defend a chunk of the market from which to expand. This book, *The Art of 'Ware*, is intended as a survival guide for such firms. While ostensibly written for CEOs and company presidents, it actually has value for company employees at all levels, as well as investors, consultants, and analysts. By understanding the princi-

1

ples given here, you increase your value to the firm(s) with which you are associated. By applying these principles, you increase the likelihood of survival for both your company and your job. Failure to do so can mean failure indeed.

Origins

The Art of Ware is based on an ancient work of Chinese literature entitled *Suntzu pingfa*, or simply *Suntzu*, generally known in English as *Sun Tzu's The Art of War*. These writings are named after and attributed to a fifth century B.C. Chinese general named Sun Wu, more commonly known as Sun Tzu (Master Sun). He, too, lived at a time of upheaval, change, and intrigue, a time when the Zhou empire was slowly dissolving into a multitude of competing regions, city-states, and clans, a time that came to be known as the Warring States period.

Suntzu pingfa is directed primarily to the general in charge of an army, though some advice is aimed at the rulers to whom the general reports. Through the ages, the book has been prized not just for its military value, but for the deeper issues of conflict, humanity, wisdom, loyalty, and risk upon which it touches. Here are some of Sun Tzu's more famous maxims (taken from the 1910 English translation by Lionel Giles):

All warfare is based on deception.

When you surround an army, leave an outlet free.

To fight and conquer in all your battles is not supreme excellence; supreme excellence consists in breaking the enemy's resistance without fighting.

It is precisely when a force has fallen into harm's way that it is capable of striking a blow for victory.

Format

In *Suntzu pingfa*, each chapter (there are thirteen in all) covers a particular topic, giving a set of maxims with advice on military matters. Throughout the centuries, various commentators interpreted or expanded upon these maxims, or gave historical examples illustrating them.

This book follows the same structure, the same number of chapters, and the same order of topics as *Suntzu pingfa*. The maxims within each chapter have been rephrased with the intent of describing how to succeed at developing and marketing technology. Again, the order of ideas has been largely preserved, with the appropriate updating. However, in some cases I have combined, rearranged, or eliminated maxims to produce a more logical organization or to avoid redundancy.

Most maxims are followed by brief commentary expanding upon or clarifying the concept being presented. Since my background is primarily in the computer industry, that's where my examples are drawn from, but the principles can be applied in many different industries and to business in general.

At the end of the book, I've given a bibliography of current English translations of *Suntzu pingfa*. I've also listed contemporary books that I feel have important things to say about the topics covered here.

Content

There is a natural translation that occurs in going from Sun Tzu's time to ours: generals become CEOs, rulers are the boards of directors, soldiers transform into developers and marketers, the landscape is the marketplace, and enemy forces become simply the competition. But that mapping, except on the simplest level, is anything but mechanical. Indeed, the challenge time and again was to come up with an appropriate parallel that directly reflects all of what Sun Tzu had to say, yet is meaningful for the topic at hand and sustains itself throughout several maxims, a chapter, or even the entire book.

There is little in here of development methodologies or management theories, just as *Suntzu pingfa* seldom talks about how to organize an army or which weapons to use. If Sun Tzu had focused on those details, his writings would have been quickly dated; instead, by eliciting underlying principles and truths, he left timeless advice. Likewise, my hope is that by avoiding current fads or theories, this book can offer broad application and age gracefully in an industry that is constantly reinventing itself.

Lacking 2,000 years to circulate galleys, I have been forced to provide the simple commentary that follows most maxims, drawing upon some 15 years of involvement in the computer industry, including direct contribution to over a dozen commercial products. However, to help this book live up to both the spirit and intent of *Suntzu pingfa*, I am soliciting commentary—for possible inclusion in subsequent editions—from those of you who want to expand upon, provide examples for, or rebut the maxims presented. For more details, see the section entitled "An Invitation" starting on page 157.

Intent

I confess to a fair amount of soul searching while working on *The Art of 'Ware*. It made me face directly how much of our economy is based on zero-sum competition: company A gains only to the extent that company B loses. This naturally leads to William Davidow's blunt statement from *Marketing High Technology*: "Crush the competition." Such an approach is usually justified in terms of economic Darwinism, implying that the result will be the best products at the best prices for the consumer. Unfortunately, the result is often entrenched mediocrity and success of the lowest common denominator, as is seen in many segments of the industry today.

Sun Tzu has a profound moral tone in his writings, and his fundamental approach is that conflict is the last resort. Still, the advice given here does tell how to inflict economic punishment upon another company. I know firsthand the costs and consequences of such damage: twice I've been laid off as part of a company reduction-in-force, or RIF (a phrase and acronym that comes from the U.S. military, by the way); once the company I worked for shut down altogether. Each RIF was a response to reduced sales and profits caused by strong competition; those same factors have been behind the rolling layoffs across the industry and throughout the national economy for the last few years. As the joke goes, what's the status symbol of the 1990s? A job.

Many established companies already apply the principles in this book. For example, I've gained a healthy respect for Bill Gates' business and marketing acumen: much of what I had found inexplicable in Microsoft's success, or had attributed to luck, I see now as the result of diligent application of many of the principles described by Sun Tzu.

Most successful innovations come from small companies, as do most failures. It's quite common for a small firm to come up with a great new idea and fail at marketing it, after which the larger firms pick among the bones for the good parts, which are often poorly grafted into their own products or quietly disposed of.

My hope, then, is that this book will serve as an equalizer, that it will help the smaller companies to survive and thrive in the midst of the larger, more established, and more powerful ones. If this does happen, it will reward innovation, decentralize market and technology control, and make the free market a bit freer in the industries that—for better or for worse—will shape the nature and quality of our lives well into the 21st century.

Chapter 1

Starting Out

Many companies start out with a neat idea. They put together a great demo or presentation. They attract hot people. They raise big money. They start development. And then somewhere along the line, things go wrong. The product never ships, or customers don't like it, or someone comes out with a better version. Money runs short. People leave. Other firms acquire the technology, or maybe just copy the ideas. The company lingers, is absorbed or dies. And the cycle starts all over again. True, this does make for a steady stream of new and interesting jobs. But there's got to be a better way.

In the first chapter of Suntzu pingfa, Sun Tzu discusses the five factors that govern competition, the means for sizing up which of two competing sides has an advantage, and how to deceive, confuse, and manipulate your opponent. The key point: unless you understand all this before you start, you're likely to fail in the end.

Product development is vital to the company; it defines the landscape of success and failure, the road to growth or collapse. It must be thoroughly studied.

Every company has a *product*: that which it produces, sells, or exchanges. The product may be something physical, some form of information, some service, or a combination of the three. Product development, then, includes the entire cycle of conception, design, and production of a finished product; in its most general sense, it also includes marketing and selling the product.

So, what is *success*? I'm tempted to paraphrase an old quote: I may not be able to define it, but I know it when I see it. The same is true with failure.

The closest working definition I've come up with for success is achieving the goals of your company, its employees, and its investors (including stockholders, if any). Of course, there may be a lot of different and even incompatible goals in that group. That's why success is relative. In the view of shareholders, former General Dynamics CEO William Anders helped achieve tremendous success, because General Dynamics stock increased dramatically in value. On the other hand, many former GD employees feel angry and betrayed because tens of thousands of them were laid off as Anders sold off, scaled back, or closed down entire divisions, earning for himself tens of millions of dollars in bonuses linked to stock performance. In their view, General Dynamics has failed. Both viewpoints are defensible; it all depends upon where you sit.

This may all seem self-evident, a review of Econ 101 mixed in with the latest issue of *Forbes*. But it's so hard to succeed and so easy to fail. I know—I've been on both sides. All things considered, I prefer to succeed, and I prefer as many people involved as possible to succeed.

These factors govern the success of the company: Tao; the economy; the marketplace; leadership; management.

Tao means running the company so that all the employees share the same vision of success.

This is probably the single most difficult concept—and task—introduced in this book. Why? Because it is hard to achieve success for a diverse group of people, and the more people involved, the harder it gets. Universal stock options help, but they are not by themselves sufficient.

It is also difficult because there is a moral element involved. For Tao to be achieved, there has to be an outstanding level of reciprocal dedication, loyalty, and trust between the employees of the company at all levels. This does not mean that employees are not accountable to their managers or vice versa; quite the contrary. But there is a Taoist paradox at the heart of this: the manager must focus on the needs of the employee, while the employee must focus on the needs of the company. This is a powerful situation, since each acts as the other's advocate, each helps the other to succeed, and each trusts the intentions of the other.

It breaks down, of course, if that mutual advocacy isn't there. When both manager and employee place the needs of the company as paramount, the stage is set for burnout, declining quality of results, and turnover. When both place the needs of the employee as paramount, then the company suffers and, eventually, so does the employee. And the last situation—where the manager places the needs of the company first, while the employee places his or her own needs first—is the classic adversarial management-vs.-labor relationship that has been the source of tremendous conflict, inefficiency, fraud, violence, corruption, waste, and suffering since the start of the Industrial Revolution.

Does Tao guarantee success? No. Does lack of Tao guarantee failure? No. But as market forces continue to dismantle or reorganize the large corporate structures that have dominated the 20th century (and the mentalities that go with them), firms that seek to achieve and maintain Tao will have a decided advantage.

The economy means buying and selling, lending and borrowing, growth and decay.

Technology-based industries go through waves of prosperity that aren't always related to the national or global economy. This still fuels the basic dream of a small group of developers making a fortune, even though cost to market has risen tremendously and the technical economy now tracks the national economy more closely. Even so, new opportunities can turn things upside down; witness the mad, intense scramble into the Internet/Web marketplace, a development that caught even Microsoft by surprise, and the fortunes made at Netscape's IPO.

The economic aspect of product development has to do with cash flow for the company itself: how much money (or credit) is on hand, what the monthly "burn rate" of resources is, what additional sources exist, what additional expenses are required or anticipated, what the bottom line is each and every month, and how well future income and expenses can be predicted.

New companies typically must raise sufficient capital to complete an initial product and then successfully bring it to market. That capital may be from sweat equity, personal savings, contract work, advance royalties, private investment, corporate partnerships, or venture firms. Each of these sources has its advantages and its costs; failure to understand these trade-offs can lead a bright young company to the point where it carries the heavy burden of development and marketing without much in the way of rewards.

The marketplace means time to market, ease of development, potential demand, customer requirements, competition, and return on investment.

Success depends upon how quickly and cheaply you can bring to market a product that people are willing to buy in sufficient quantities. This means that you've got to understand both what it is you're trying to build and who is going to choose to spend their money on it instead of on something else, including equivalent products from other firms. Beyond that, you have to be able to sell your products for a price at which you can make a profit—not just pay back what you spent coming to market, but actually show a return on that original investment. And you have to do this in an arena filled with companies that are better staffed, better funded, and better known than yours.

Leadership means the qualities of wisdom, integrity, humanity, vision, and fairness.

Wisdom means knowing the right thing to do, and the right reason for doing it. *Integrity* represents the ethical and moral dimensions of business that are sometimes neglected in executive offices, particularly those of sales and marketing. *Humanity* involves remembering that every decision made affects people's lives—including those in competing firms. *Vision* is the quality of seeing beyond the next quarter's results and into the future. *Fairness* mixes compassion, justice, and evenhandedness appropriately.

These qualities are uncommon, and are seldom found in equal and sufficient proportions in a single person. But that does not excuse their absence, nor does it relieve us of the effort to achieve them. They must reside in those who lead the company, and they must be expected of employees at all levels.

Management means organization, communication, acquisition of resources, and budgeting.

Many start-ups are run by technical or visionary individuals who do not fully understand or appreciate the role of management in a successful company. This can lead to failure to recognize or reward contributions, exhaustion of resources, inefficient use of time, and even legal problems. Management skills should be as important in a company, division, or product group as technical skills.

By answering these seven questions, you can judge ahead of time how well the company will succeed:

Does the board of directors have Tao?

The common image is that the directors are only interested in the bottom line. But a board that is collectively committed to the company vision can be a powerful force for good: when they have to ask the difficult questions, they do so for the right reasons. There are boards like that, and they benefit the companies they advise.

Does the CEO offer true leadership?

Leadership is the quality of setting a direction that encompasses the charter of the company, then guiding the employees to that end. True leadership must be built upon integrity, or it will ultimately fail.

How well does the company adapt to the economy and to the marketplace?

Because of the long path that often winds from original idea to shipping product, the company needs to be willing and able to adapt to changes in the economy and in the marketplace as it goes along. This becomes ever more critical as the rate of change in the technical markets continues to pick up speed.

As importantly, the company needs to be able to complete and launch products successfully. This requires marketing acumen, sufficient capital, and a product that meets the needs and demands of the customers, not of the engineers, the marketers, or the management.

How excellent are the management skills?

Management is the art of increasing communication, reducing friction, and achieving goals. Superior management comes from below, as managers see themselves serving and supporting those they supervise.

How committed are the employees?

Leadership, management, and Tao are essential in having the employees commit to see the process through. Stock options and profit sharing don't hurt, but they will not long compensate for lack of management or leadership.

How skilled are the developers?

The "infinite number of monkeys" approach doesn't work for technology development. You are better off having a few excellent engineers than a lot of mediocre or inexperienced ones. In many cases, you're better off having just a few excellent engineers than a lot of excellent engineers. Why? Communication, coordination, and unity of product architecture.

How much opportunity is there for growth and how little tolerance for incompetence?

Excellent developers and marketers don't change jobs to do the same old thing; they change jobs to do something new. Keeping excellent engineers means giving them the chance to grow professionally.

On the other hand, one unwilling or misdirected developer or marketer can tie up significant resources. Make it clear when someone is hired that competence, cooperation, and hard work are prerequisites to keeping their job. I once had the awkward experience of having to fire a friend whom I had hired for a development project because I felt he was unwilling or unable to complete the tasks assigned to him. I'm afraid the friendship didn't survive the experience.

Even with all these qualities in place, you must still look for or create opportunities to use them.

No matter how well managed a company is, without something of value to sell, it will go nowhere. A perfectly organized and managed company cannot sell a product the customers won't buy.

Successful product development requires stealth and misdirection. Hide your strengths at first and appear to be weak; when actively developing, show no signs.

Any concept, once viewed, can be imitated, in appearance if not in fact. There is a real danger in exposing product concepts too quickly, though it is a risk that sometimes must be taken to raise capital. Likewise, you don't want to tip off your competition as to what you're doing, unless there's an advantage in doing so.

Managing external perceptions and expectations while developing a new product is a difficult task. Revealing too much too soon can raise expectations too high while giving your competition a clear view as to what you're doing.

If product release will be soon, make it appear to be far away; if product release is far in the future, make it appear to be imminent.

With the first approach, you can lull competitors into complacency and lower the expectations of consumers. In both areas, the advantage of a sooner-than-expected release can be tremendous.

The second approach is the classic FUD strategy: fear, uncertainty, and doubt. This tactic was honed to a fine art by IBM and has since been adopted with success by Microsoft, particularly with regard to each successive version of Windows. The danger is loss of credibility, particularly with customers and the press, but it may work to freeze or misdirect the competition.

Entice the competition into a market segment, then confuse them by your response. Where they are focused, strengthen yourself. Where they are successful, avoid them.

It helps to have a market niche that you are prepared to grant your competitors, particularly one that they would be interested in anyway. Talk it up, lure them in, then go elsewhere where your real strengths are.

Build strong walls where your competitors might intrude on your market share. Don't waste resources attempting to win committed customers away from them.

Annoy their leaders to irritate and distract them. Hide your advantages to make them take you lightly.

Feuding CEOs are a time-honored tradition in the technology industry; large egos have often prevented what might have otherwise been successful partnerships and mergers. If you can get your competitors on the defensive, or at least really ticked with you, you may be able to tempt them into doing something rash.

There's an art to making your customers (and investors) love you while having your competitors not take you seriously, but it can be done—many successful, established companies started out as small ones that weren't taken too seriously (Borland, Apple, Microsoft).

Wear the competition out by faster development.

Invest in your engineers. Take the time to give them proper training, resources, tools. Discover the secrets of rapid product development—and when you do, keep them to yourself. In the process, be sure you wear the competition out and not your own developers.

Break up competing alliances and sow internal dissensions.

Alliances between convergence companies are constantly forming and shifting. Mergers are announced almost monthly; some actually go through. "Strategic alliances" are more common, but are less significant unless resources are actually committed. Even so, if those mergers and alliances threaten your company, you should find ways to undermine them.

Likewise, when it is in your interest, look for ways to cause disagreements within a competing firm over product and market direction (see Chapter 12, "Competing by Influence"). This will slow them down and may even misdirect them.

Release products at a time and in a market which they don't expect. Do not freeze product specs and marketing approach too far in advance.

The competition will base a lot of their plans, consciously or unconsciously, on what they expect you to do. The more you surprise them, the less effective their plans will be and the less confidence they'll have in those plans.

To compete, you need product technology that allows for last-minute shifting of the final specification and target market without the months of delay such changes usually entail. Companies that achieve this will have a better chance of surviving the rapid technology turnover in the industry.

Those who create an honest and well-thought-out business plan will likely succeed. Those who don't will likely fail.

Too many business plans are an exercise in creative writing. This is often done to convince others to invest in a company, an effort of dubious ethical and practical results. The greatest danger, though, is when you believe the fantasy yourself.

Beyond that, your plan for business must be something far beyond the traditional written business plan. You must systematically address the issues raised in this chapter at the very start and lay the groundwork for success from the beginning. Otherwise, you risk wasting the time and/or money of all involved.

While success may depend in part upon luck—that is, upon events and circumstances outside your control—it remains a truism that fortune favors the prepared. This chapter covered the ways in which you can prepare for success. Any resistance you and others feel towards considering these issues and questions in detail should be a warning flag.

Chapter 2

Supporting Development

A parable in the Bible talks about counting the cost of something before you start to build. That truth is ancient and obvious, yet I've seen too many companies ignore it. Once you know what you want to do, you have to figure out how to do it—and particularly how much it's going to cost. Resources required include people, money, time, mindshare, technology, and information. They are all expended as development proceeds, and not all are renewable.

Sun Tzu talks in his second chapter about the resource issues of mobilizing troops and waging war. What's important, he says, is to succeed as soon as possible; the longer things drag out, the worse the results, regardless of how much "better" the product. If you don't believe me, just ask anyone (else) who has shipped a product a year late.

19

Product development requires a core development team, support and quality engineers, and the necessary resources from production and marketing.

It is still possible for an outstanding concept, technology, or product to be designed and developed by a few people working in a garage or a cheap office. What is almost impossible is for those same few people to bring the product to market on their own. Customer expectations of quality—in marketing, packaging, documentation, customer support, and, of course, the product itself—are at a very high level, and there are a lot of fiercely competitive companies that can provide that level of quality.

The cost of supporting these employees for 18-24 months, including recruiting, salary, training, travel, marketing, and money spent on equipment, office space, utilities, and supplies, will amount to roughly $8,000 per month per person. Such is the price of new product development.

This figure is less in some places with lower wages and cost of living (say, Utah or Russia). And, of course, things can be done a bit cheaper in a start-up, particularly if the developers are fresh out of college. But that $8,000/month figure—about $100,000 per year—is a good, conservative rule of thumb, especially for business planning.

Will this figure change in the future? Yes, but slowly, since wage inflation isn't very high right now.

When you release a product, if success is slow in coming, you'll face diminishing returns on product development and exhaustion among your engineers and marketers.

It is enough of a challenge to sustain energy and excitement through the process of actually getting the product out the door. If returns are slow and small, people can get discouraged and start looking for the door themselves.

When your developers are burned out, your technology aging, your resources diminished, and your advantages gone, then others will take advantage of your weaknesses and cut into your market. Even expensive consultants and new CEOs won't be able to turn things around.

Few technology companies manage to keep themselves in a lead position for more than five years. At that point, they usually become victims of their own success. The visionaries who founded the company are either gone or given emeritus status. Market focus is on adding yet more features to old, bloated products; no one is willing to risk coming up with new products and technologies that might cannibalize existing ones. And so they start on the long (or, sometimes, not so long) glide downwards, shedding products and people, sometimes merging with other firms on the downward slope. Some companies manage to level off, or at least to slow the rate of descent, but they rarely regain their former status; their place in the market has been filled by other companies with newer products and technologies.

There have been product releases that were poorly done but quickly successful, but there have been few that were well-executed and that took a long time to succeed. No company has benefitted from a prolonged competition.

There are three dangers in a prolonged competition. First, it consumes resources that could be applied to new markets and products. Second, it narrows your profit margin, further limiting resources that could be applied elsewhere. Third, it tends to lock you in on your current products, blocking development of new ones and leaving you vulnerable to new competitors.

Note, though, that success is relative. In established markets, there are typically two to four major players who between them own 90% of the market. In such a case, gaining even a few percentage points of market share is cause for celebration; witness the fierce battles between Pepsi and Coca-Cola for mere fractions of a point.

Those who don't understand all the issues and risks in product development and release cannot understand the best techniques to be used.

Many books have been written about these issues and risks; the single best summary is *The Mythical Man-Month*, written by Frederick P. Brooks. Written over 20 years ago and recently updated, it is dead on in its explanations about why projects fail or, at least, are late and over budget. There is more than enough blame to go around: engineers, project managers, marketing folks, and upper-level executives. It should be mandatory reading for every single employee in a technology venture, as well as any associated investors and directors.

Those who handle product development skillfully don't build engineering teams twice, nor raise capital three times.

Building product development teams twice means having to replace the original engineers with new ones in order to complete the product. There can be any number of reasons for having to do this: the engineers get burned out; the engineers get disgusted with upper management and leave; the engineers lose faith in the company and its directions, particularly if they view the product as being "hijacked" and taken in a different direction by latecomers to the company; or the engineers are replaced and/or fired, either because of insubordination or because they weren't the right ones for the job in the first place.

Raising capital three times before product release indicates that development and launch have taken too long. (Believe me, I know.) The first round is usually essential to get the company off the ground. The second round may be necessary because of changes in product direction or the all-too-common delays in product development. But you're in trouble if you raise a third round of capital for anything but product launch, and possibly even then. Not only does it mean that you're late in shipping, it also means that you're surrendering equity—thus reducing equity incentives for existing employees—and that you do not have sufficient cash reserves to keep the company going once the product does finally ship.

Focus on creating your own development resources, and recruit from your competition. This way, you can be sufficient in both tools and personnel.

Invest in development resources, that is, the tools needed to actually create the product. All the money you can think of possibly spending on those resources probably won't equal what you'll lose each and every month your product is late. Likewise, be willing to devote people and resources to creating custom in-house development resources. It's easy to choose not to do this, because you can often "get by" without such tools and you may be concerned about the return on investment. But the right tools can make a significant difference in product quality and time to completion.

Some of the best people to do your product development are at other companies and are probably at your competitors. Recruit aggressively and hire the best, strengthening yourself and weakening your competition.

When a company is drained by competition, it is because product development and marketing have taken too long. Prolonged development cripples the company.

Developers can typically sustain a high level of energy for 18 to 36 months, depending upon how hard they're being pressed. After that, they start looking around for something new to work on. A project that takes too long getting out the door runs the danger of never shipping, because key developers keep leaving to work on something else, either within the company or outside of it.

There are other significant internal and external problems caused by prolonged development. People within the company begin to lose heart, bicker, and find fault with each other. Customers question the company's ability to deliver products in a timely fashion. Competitors use your delays against you to win customers and sow doubt about you.

Even allies begin to doubt and may seek to distance themselves from you. During the very long year between our original ship date at Pages and when our product—which was to run under NEXTSTEP—actually went out the door, someone at NeXT swore we'd never ship and said he'd eat a can of worms if we ever did. We did ship, on March 7, 1994. We never heard if this person carried out his promise; we certainly kept our end of the bargain.

In key areas of technology development, talent is scarce and salaries are high, limiting resources for other employees.

As new technologies become hot markets, the number of skilled developers is small, and they command high salaries. For example, in the software industry this has been true at various times for 8086 assembly, Windows, C++, OLE 2.0, object-oriented development, and Internet-related technologies. Each area fills in with time as sustained demand and high salaries draw more engineers into it. But, curiously enough, the absolute number of excellent developers in a given area of technology remains pretty much the same.

When I was teaching computer science at Brigham Young University in 1985–87, the number of students enrolled as computer science majors had increased dramatically—by a factor of five or so—from when I had been a student there a decade earlier. One of the professors, who had been around since the early 70s, observed to me that the number of really good students in the department was still pretty much the same; the five-fold growth of enrollment hadn't brought a five-fold, or even a two-fold, increase in excellent CS majors. Why? Because those students with interest, aptitude, and native talent had been signing up all along; the surge in enrollment had come from students who saw computers as a way to get a great paying job, much as my friends during my undergraduate days had signed up for pre-law or pre-med.

When a new area of technology opens up, it quickly draws to it those developers with the interest, talents and desire to become really good in it. More excellent developers do come along with time, but as they do, some of the current ones start moving on to new areas, so the absolute number stays more or less constant.

Because of this, I'd like to propose a minor addition to the vast assortment of laws and rules governing technology and engineering:

Webster's Constant: the number of excellent developers in a new area of technology quickly reaches a constant value, which is sustained through the period during which the technology is vital.

This may seem a bit silly or fatuous, but it's actually critical to understand if you need to build a development team that will be working with key technologies. It's going to be tough finding really good people, and you'll find yourself running into the same names over and over again. The trick is getting them to come work for you.

When funds are exhausted, then money is raised under pressure. Control is lost and equity surrendered to supply the needed resources.

One of life's great ironies is that the worst time to raise money is when you really need it, because that's when you'll have to agree to the most unfavorable terms. The logical conclusion, then, is to start working on raising money well before you need it. If you end up not needing it, so be it; but if you do, you will have done the work in advance. That's also important, because it takes time to raise money.

Try to gain resources from the competition. Each dollar gained from or spent by the competition is worth two dollars raised and spent by yourself.

You can leverage off your competition by learning from their market research, analyzing their plans and products, and buying their technology. See Chapter 13 ("Gathering Intelligence") for more details and ideas.

Reward employees who recruit from competitors. Merge those recruits with your own and win their loyalty. This is called weakening the competition while increasing your own strength.

The best people for your positions are often found at competing companies. They are often well versed both in the product areas of interest (otherwise these firms aren't competing with you) and in key areas of technology. If you're starting a new company, it may be the only place you can find them.

Your employees outperform the competition because of zeal.

If your developers had wanted to work long hours just for lots of money, they would have become lawyers. They do it for bragging rights—for the right to say, "Yeah, I helped create that product"—and for a chance to change the industry and maybe the world. It may be hubris, but then again, the world really has changed because of products created by technology developers over the last thirty to forty years—and the most dramatic changes are yet to come.

Employees create successful products because they desire reward. Therefore, reward them based on success and profits.

The previous maxim notwithstanding, developers do want some significant financial reward. Most developers dream of making enough money to go off and do what they really want to do, which often is to start their own company or to do something unrelated to the project just completed. Because of that, they are very keen on ideas such as stock options and profit sharing.

The important thing in competing is succeeding, not enduring.

Many companies have managed to endure a long time, and even provide a comfortable (if not always secure) living for those employed there. But once it becomes apparent that a company is only enduring, not succeeding, all the good people will leave, and it will be nearly impossible to turn the company around.

Many firms want a world-class development team; few are willing to make the effort and allocate the resources to create one. On the other hand, it's easy to spend a lot of money without achieving the desired results. There is an art to doing it, and you'll undoubtedly make mistakes along the way. Hey, if it were easy, everyone would do it.

Chapter 3

Sizing Up the Competition

A customer is an individual who is able and may be willing to exchange resources (usually, though not always, money) for your products. A market is a collection of customers who have needs or desires that they may believe can be satisfied by your product—or a competing equivalent. The question is, if the customer is willing to spend money, will it be for your product or for someone else's? That is the essence of competing within the marketplace.

Note that a new market can be a simple refinement of an old one: color TVs over B&W. It can be a new solution to an existing need: compact discs over vinyl records. Or it can be an entirely new technology: Internet access and presence on the World Wide Web. By controlling how markets are defined, you can sidestep or outflank competing firms.

The best, yet hardest, way to capture a market is to define a new one and flood it with a successful product. The next best way is to let someone else try to define it, learn from their mistakes, and then flood the market with a successful product. The worst, yet safest, way is to take on an entrenched, successful product in a mature market.

The focus of Sun Tzu's third chapter is that the best victory is one without fighting—but if you do have to fight, make sure you can win.

The best strategy is to capture a market without directly competing: it's far more difficult to wrest market share away from another company.

Customers are slow to change. They have made investments in their current solutions: money, time, training, skills required, media. In order to get them to risk money, their previous investments, and other resources on your product, you must convince them that it's worth the risk. So you need to make those risks as low as possible. You do that by keeping price low, preserving prior investments, and minimizing other resource requirements (again, time, training, skills required, and so on). If they see your product as complementing or working side-by-side with their current solutions, you lower those risks. If you try to make them give up the familiar for the unknown, you're in for a fight. If you can provide a compelling function, capability, or result that their current solution does not provide, you'll have a better chance, but success is by no means guaranteed.

Customers can be a pain in the butt. They are by turns capricious, illogical, self-defeating, and often quite confused about what they want vs. what they need. Of course, those who develop products often exhibit identical symptoms, so the customers can hardly be faulted for their behavior.

It's better to absorb a company than to drive it out of business. It's better to purchase a division, product, or technology than to cause it to fail. It's better to hire good developers from the competition than to make them unemployed.

By acquiring a competitor, you gain its technology, its people, its customers, and its market share. If you drive it out of business, you may gain none of these. Of course, if you're too successful, the U.S. Justice Department may raise anti-trust concerns, but in that case you know that you've already succeeded.

If you acquire a competing product, you can enhance your own, and you can woo over the customers who use the old one. If you cause it to fail, the customers will be slow to adopt yours and may actually resent you for making their lives more difficult.

If you cause the competition's best developers to lose their jobs, they will hate you and work against your company at every turn. If you recruit them away and give them good jobs, they will help you to beat their old firms.

The height of skill isn't winning head-to-head competition; it's convincing other firms not to compete at all.

Yeah, there's an ego boost in taking away market share in direct competition, but it tends to have two side effects. First, the competition most likely will pour even more resources into winning back that share, which in turn will force you to devote more resources to countering them, and so on. Second, the customers you're vying for will see what's going on, and they'll play you and your competition off of each other, driving down margins and driving up product requirements. That, of course, is the whole point of the free market; but don't forget that the free market also requires that companies fail. Your responsibility is to be sure that yours isn't one of them.

If you're a small company, position your product so that other firms see it as non threatening, or as enhancing their sales. If you're big, stake out market position preemptively so that other firms stay away. In either case, a lack of direct competition can mean higher margins and better profits.

The best approach is to disrupt your competitors' plans.

By coming out with an advanced, successful product, you can cause competing firms to change their own business and development plans before they even get started. Hiring away key management or development personnel can slow down or redirect other companies. And preemptive announcements or displays of technology can cause competitors to rethink their own strategy.

The next best approach is to undermine, usurp, or join alliances between competitors.

If you see two or more firms combining to compete against you, seek ways to blunt the impact of that alliance. You can do this by forming your own competing alliance with other firms; by establishing relationships with individual firms in the competing alliance; or by joining the alliance yourself, then directing it on a course that coincides with your interests.

The constantly shifting alliances of the past few years, particularly in the convergence industries, aren't necessarily a sign of confusion or chaos. They often reflect the sharp competition and market collisions of the major players in the industry. On the other hand, they sometimes *are* a sign of confusion and chaos, and it's not always easy to tell the difference.

The next best approach is to beat a competing development effort to market.

Success can often depend as much upon timing as upon quality or functionality. Often, the first application aimed at a given market will have a major advantage over latecomers, all other things being more or less equal. Thus, Microsoft Word for Windows captured a larger market share than WordPerfect for Windows, even though WordPerfect/DOS had a commanding lead over Microsoft Word/DOS.

Even so, this is a more difficult approach, since you will end up with head-to-head competition. Worse yet, you may simply clear a path for the competition to follow in behind you with a better product, answering your customers' needs better than you do.

The worst approach is to directly attack an established product; do this only when you have no other choice.

A direct attack means seeking to take customers away from an existing product that they already use or that they might choose over yours to accomplish the same task. To convince customers to switch, you need to present an overwhelming advantage; otherwise, they will be unwilling to surrender their investment in money, skill, familiarity, and trust. That advantage usually takes the form of lower prices, which makes it harder for your firm to pour money back into marketing for improved sales and into R&D for new and better products.

If you're attacking an established product, take sufficient time to prepare your product and your marketing.

A direct attack on an established product requires careful planning, while your own product must be well designed and of compelling interest. Much thought needs to be given as to how to best position your product (and the competition's). Typically, this involves a combination of low cost, strong advantages for switching, and some degree of compatibility with existing solutions.

If you release the product into the market prematurely, spending money and revealing direction and technology without gaining significant market share, then you'll have a disastrous product release.

A product that is rushed to market still having significant bugs or lacking important features, or that is pushed out into the market without an intelligent, coordinated marketing plan in place, will fail in the face of decent competition (including competition from earlier versions of the same product).

An excellent CEO will leapfrog others' development efforts, gain market share without direct competition, and quickly convince competing firms to go elsewhere.

Here, then, are the three keys to success:

* Introduce products that have a compelling advantage over competing products: price, performance, features, or a combination of the three.
* When possible, aim your product at those who have not yet adopted your competitors' products, building market position in anticipation of drawing customers away from your competitors.
* Establish a position that compels your competitors to avoid direct competition with you and to seek other markets.

You must compete on all levels for complete success, so that your profits are maximized and your resources are not tied up. This is the art of capturing the market.

Market capture occurs when you best others by strategy, rather than by direct competition. You spend less money, reap greater profits, and better preserve the energy and enthusiasm of your developers and marketers.

Here are the rules for direct competition, based on how your product stacks up against the entrenched competition.

These rules are going to talk about how much "better" your product is than those against which you're competing. Let me say this loud and clear: **"better" is entirely in the eye of the customer**. It is absolutely critical that you base these rules on how actual live customers rate your product, not on what you think of it. And that rating has to be based primarily on their willingness and ability to spend money, forego some or all of their investment in current solutions, and change their current way of doing things. That will depend on several factors: the product itself, how you position it, what the customers' needs and wants are, what the costs of adoption are, and who else is using it (i.e., how "standard" it is). You may have the best product on the market, but unless the customers are willing to buy it, it doesn't matter.

Do not fall into the trap of believing your own hype about your product, nor what reviewers say, nor even what customers say absent the commitment of a purchase order or a check. Yes, all those things can help keep up internal and external enthusiasm. But in the end, all that matters is whether people buy your product in quantities sufficient to warrant the original investment. If not, then your product wasn't truly a "better" solution than what customers were already using.

If your product is ten times better, absorb the competing product's market.

A vastly superior product—in the sense defined above—will be able to take over an inferior product's market and customer base and, in fact, will draw in customers who never accepted the inferior product. You don't even need to mention the inferior product in your ads; just tout your own advantages, and let the market do the rest.

If five times better, attack competing products directly.

With a five-fold advantage, you can capture significant market share with a direct campaign. Mention your benefits and the competition's weaknesses. As you gain momentum and market share, you can set yourself up to absorb the competition's market (see previous item).

If twice as good, carve out market segments.

If your product is only twice as good, then you need to create new market segments where your competition is weak. By building up market share in those segments, you can position yourself for a move into other segments occupied by your competition (see previous item). Why? Because installed base is itself a factor in making a product better; the more people who use your product, the "better" your product is (again, in the sense we're using here).

If just as good, look for open market segments to go after.

See where your competition doesn't sell, then go there. In the process, build a loyal customer base against the day when your competition comes into your segments. At the same time, use this as a base for carving out new market segments (see previous item).

If not quite as good, then avoid competing with it.

You must find areas your competition doesn't want, such as low cost, and then stay with them. If your competition starts to move in, then find new areas, unless you've built up enough of a loyal following to resist incursion (see previous item).

If much worse, then find another market (and another product).

There is seldom any point in seeking to market a product that is much worse than the competition. Your return on investment will usually be low, and your competition will be able to easily move in and take market share away from you. Indeed, you will end up doing marketing for them by establishing the need without adequately fulfilling it.

If a small firm is stubborn and does not follow these guidelines, it will lose to the larger firm.

All things being equal, or when the smaller firm has a better product, the larger firm will usually beat out the smaller firm. The flip side of this is that a large firm can bend or stretch these guidelines, but not always.

The CEO leads and directs the company. When that leadership is complete, the company is strong; when it is defective or unsure, the company is weak.

The power and moral authority to lead the company must reside in the CEO. If the CEO does not exercise wise, just, and proper leadership, the whole company suffers, regardless of its other advantages.

There are three ways in which directors and investors can cause problems for the company:

If directors incorrectly force or hinder development of a given product, they damage the development process.

If the directors bypass the CEO and try to dictate the pace and aim of product development, they undermine the CEO's leadership and may force the CEO into unwise development and marketing decisions.

If directors bypass the company leaders and attempt to manage the company, employees become confused.

Again, management must be left to the CEO and senior managers. Not only does such intervention by the board undermine the CEO, but directors seldom understand all the issues involved, nor do they have to live with the immediate consequences.

If directors don't understand the development process, yet attempt to dictate development methodology and schedule, developers become frustrated and angry.

Perhaps the worst micromanagement that directors can be guilty of is trying to tell the developers how to develop the product. The directors will most likely be wrong, and they will drive the best developers away from the company.

There are five ways of knowing which CEOs will lead their company to success.

Those who know when and when not to compete will succeed.

The CEO needs to be able to assess the competition and to judge their relative strengths and weaknesses. From this, the CEO can judge whether or not to compete.

Those who know whether to allocate many or few marketing resources to a given product will succeed.

Not all products are of equal value. Some will yield an acceptable return for a small investment; others will require a large investment, but will yield a great return.

Those whose managers and developers share the same vision will succeed.

The CEO must truly lead by developing and sharing a vision with all others in a company. When all employees share a vision, then the company can succeed.

Those who face unprepared competitors with preparation will succeed.

The wise CEO anticipates both markets and competition and then plans accordingly; if the competition is not as prepared, then the company can succeed.

Those who are skilled and not micromanaged by the directors will succeed.

The CEO must know how to run the company according to the principles above, yet must be able to keep the directors happy with the progress and direction of the company so that the directors don't seek to micromanage.

If you understand the competition's products and also your own, then you won't be at risk in most product releases.

By understanding the products from both firms, you know how to position yours according to its relative strengths and weaknesses, as described above; thus, you can minimize the risk at each product release.

If you're not familiar with the competition's products, but you do understand your own products well, then you'll succeed about half the time.

Failure to understand your competition's products can lead you to misposition your own; however, understanding your own allows you to market it to its best advantage.

If you don't understand either your products or those of the competition, then you'll fail most of the time.

It's hard to see how you could succeed in such a case, except because of brilliant subordinates or sheer dumb luck. Of course, both circumstances have been known to happen, but they're not a proposition worth betting upon.

Direct competition, like direct combat, is painful, costly, destructive, and often yields a low return for all that is expended. It also produces everimproving products at ever-decreasing prices. This is great for consumers but not so much fun for the companies involved. You should, then, seek to minimize head-to-head competition except when your advantage is overwhelming. The marketplace is littered with the husks of companies that won Pyrrhic victories over their rivals.

Chapter 4

Approaching the Market

OK, so you don't have the market to yourself. You have to worry about the competition, not to mention the customers. How well have you thought through all the possibilities? How will the competition react? How will the customers react? Are you being overly optimistic in your sales projections? Will you really achieve your planned revenue 120 days after product launch?

There's a real temptation to push your product out onto the market and wing it from there. That approach succeeds just often enough to keep us doing it. But the successes are all that we see; most failures are quick, quiet, and invisible. If we saw them as clearly as we see the successes, we'd be a lot more thoughtful and prepared in releasing a new product.

Sun Tzu, in his fourth chapter, talks about how the general must control the situation before conflict even begins. Unless the general understands both his own strategy and that of his enemy, his approach to battle is in doubt before it is even begun.

First, carefully build a strong position while looking for weaknesses in the competition.

There is no point in bringing a product to market unless it can stand on its own merits. It must be compelling enough to convince customers to spend money on it. Having defined the product's attributes and strengths, you can then examine the competition to see if there are weak areas that can be exploited.

A CEO is responsible for the company's strength; competitors, for their own weaknesses. You can make your company strong, but cannot make competitors weak.

You can control (or at least influence) research, product development, and marketing in your own company. However, you have much less influence over the competition and cannot count on them being worse than they actually are.

Indeed, there is a strong and dangerous temptation within a firm to underestimate the competition, to assume that they'll make the wrong moves or that they don't understand all that you do. This usually results in a series of unpleasant surprises as the competition does exactly the right things necessary to counter or undermine your efforts.

You may even see how to succeed without being able to do so.

Put simply, a brilliant and/or superior product can fail if the competition is just too strong. It can also fail if the customers don't need or want it: look at what happened to the slide-rule market after the introduction of pocket calculators, or to the vinyl record industry after the introduction of compact discs.

A defensive posture is for protecting market share during times of weakness; an aggressive approach is for direct competition during times of strength.

You maintain market share by convincing your customers that your product is superior (or at least good enough) and that the costs and risks of adopting a competing product are too high.

You enter a defensive, entrenching posture when pressed by a competitor with a superior product, superior marketing, or both, or when your company is having significant problems. The danger: if you are perceived as being in a defensive posture, the market will interpret it as a sign of weakness and instability, and it may further erode your position.

You gain market share by attacking competing products and convincing the customer that the costs and risks of choosing (or staying with) a competing product are too high, or that the costs and risks of adopting or trying your product are low.

When you have the upper hand in terms of product and marketing, you can choose your course and compel the competition to react accordingly. In the game of Go, this is known as *sente*: your opponent must respond to each move you make, leaving you free to choose each new move.

Entrench the product so as to resist all attacks; view the market from a high level, rapidly moving into new market opportunities as you see them. By doing this, you can protect the company while gaining market share.

There are two parts to this approach. First, you need to focus on defending your market share against all comers. Look for ways to so entrench your product and technology with customers that they will resist all competing solutions. The classic—if overused—examples of this approach are IBM (in the 1960s) and Microsoft (in the 1990s).

Second, you need to be looking for additional opportunities. New market segments and niches open up on a regular basis, and it's often a while before anyone notices. Keep thinking of new ways to apply existing technology, or new technologies that can be developed to coincide with the opening of a future market. IBM pretty much failed at this, but Microsoft has been quite aggressive and forward-looking in searching out new technologies and markets.

Many successful companies have done so with such apparent ease that their achievements are downplayed. The CEOs of such firms are seldom credited with either skill, brilliance, or courage. Still, their successes are not by accident or luck. They set things up to succeed before they ever competed, and they found ways ahead of time to make their competitors fail.

Speaking of Microsoft, it has only been in the past few years that Bill Gates has been credited with being anything but a lucky nerd. Frankly, it probably would have been to his benefit to continue to be so underestimated; he has become a lightning rod for unpleasant attention from the press, not to mention the Justice Department, and fear of Gates has formed unlikely alliances among his competitors.

Likewise, many previous successes of the computer industry—the Apple II, VisiCalc, MS-DOS, Lotus 1-2-3, Turbo Pascal, dBase, WordPerfect—are dismissed as being due to luck or just filling the right need at the right time. Yet those who succeeded had what it took to be in that right place at that right time with the right product. Witness the number of people and firms who had similar opportunities and did not succeed.

A successful company first sets up the conditions for success, then goes into the marketplace; an unsuccessful company dives into the marketplace, then tries to determine what it must do to succeed.

Often a tremendous amount of time and money is poured into product development, and it is only after the product has been launched that you try to find customers. At that point, you discover what it is that customers really wanted, which often is something quite different from what you developed. Product launch is then followed by product revisions and repositioning in an effort to gain acceptance and sales, and that is often followed by downsizing, assimilation, and evaporation. The entire history of the "pen computing" market, with tens of millions of dollars poured into Momenta, Go, EO, and others, bears eloquent witness of the dangers of building a product with no customers.

A much better approach is to ensure that customers will want what you have to sell before your product is ever released. That is not as easy as it sounds, because what customers say they want is often quite different from what customers are willing to adopt and buy. Furthermore, if you're selling to a large organization, you often have to satisfy different people with different desires and expectations. Users want something more convenient and powerful, but not that different from what they're currently using. Managers want something that will improve the bottom line. Information systems (IS) people don't want anything new or different unless it's completely compatible with existing solutions.

Those skilled in product development and marketing cultivate Tao and build their company upon strong principles. That way, they succeed where companies looking for shortcuts fail.

In the technology industries, the half-life of products, concepts, and technologies is short. As noted elsewhere, the distance from the leading edge to the trailing edge is getting smaller. Because of that, it is as important to build a team that can adapt and compete as it is to build products. It is still critical to build products; "think tank" companies seldom make a decent return on investment. But the customers themselves are a moving target, so it is likewise critical that you build a team that can do course corrections in the middle of product development without bickering, starting turf wars, or losing significant time.

There are five keys to successful product development and marketing:

measurement of market size, both current and potential:

The trick here is not to deceive yourself or to be deceived by overly optimistic predictions of the market size. Many CEOs look at vast markets out there (installed PCs, houses wired for cable, etc.) and play the 5% game: "If we capture just 5% of the market, we'll be successful!" Market share isn't based solely on the number of possible customers for your product: that's merely the upper limit. The lower limit can be pretty small indeed—close to zero in many cases. Market projections must be based on bottom-up projections, not on some hypothetical percentage of the total market.

assessment of competing products and likely market share:

Several questions help you to further lower the upper bound on potential market share. First, how many people have a need or desire for the solution you offer? Second, what percentage of those do not yet have an acceptable solution (such as a competing product)? Third, what percentage of those have the money to purchase your product? Fourth, what percentage of those would rather spend that money on your product than on any of the other myriad things they could buy with it, especially competing products?

calculations of cash flow, capital, and return on investment:

You can have significant success in the marketplace and still lose money: it just depends on whether you spend more or less money than you bring in. (Car makers demonstrate this all the time, as do various divisions of IBM.) You can make a profit and still not have enough capital to further development and marketing. You can make a profit, grow the company, and still never create an acceptable return on the initial and subsequent investments.

comparisons of different market approaches:

There are various ways of marketing a given product; success lies in knowing or discovering what they might be, in evaluating feasibility and potential results, and in choosing one or more approaches that will work.

success in product releases.

The issue affecting the bottom line is product acceptance upon release. Many companies with promising technology have stumbled or even failed because of slow market penetration.

Also, you only get one chance to make a first impression. The reputation that a product gets on initial release, deserved or not, can linger for years. Witness Apple's stumble with the Newton handheld computer.

Success comes from accurate comparisons, which come from accurate calculations, which come from accurate assessments, which come from accurate data, which come from accurate market research.

The same data, more or less, is out there for everyone. Success comes from gathering accurate information, interpreting it, making plans based on it, and choosing from among those plans.

There is a dangerous temptation to make self-serving assumptions in this process; reality will always intrude, sooner or later, and it's usually unpleasant when it happens.

Thus, a successful company compares to an unsuccessful one like a boulder colliding with a tumbleweed. When factors are lined up correctly beforehand, the successful company bursts into the marketplace like a flash flood.

A successful company can push through problems and obstacles, using its momentum and resources to carry it past the rough spots. An unsuccessful company gets hung up, blocked, or diverted easily.

Evaluation, coordination, cooperation, and timing are all essential. To make all factors mesh is difficult and rare, or else everyone would do it. Again, it is the responsibility of the CEO to see that it happens, but it is the responsibility of everyone else in the company to see that it works.

Chapter 5

Using Momentum and Timing

Something about the technology industries brings out superlative efforts, exemplified by the legendary t-shirts of the original Apple Macintosh development team: "Working 90 hours a week and lovin' it!" I've been there myself: on two different development projects, a decade apart, I had weeks where I put in over 100 hours, sometimes working 40 hours at a stretch.

But the effort this chapter focuses on is a broader, more profound type: that which makes a company push through all obstacles, bringing success after success. Circumstances align, things fall into place, and everyone is suddenly talking about and—better yet—buying your product.

In his fifth chapter, Sun Tzu uses various metaphors to represent the energy of troops in combat: a rushing torrent, a crossbow at the moment of release, a large boulder dropping down a mountain. Those same images apply today.

There should be few differences between running a small company and running a large one; it's a matter of organizing into divisions and of establishing proper communications and procedures.

We often excuse certain behaviors and practices because of the company size. In a small company, we are tempted to be less than rigorous with finances and professional standards. In a large company, we often substitute policy manuals for leadership and politics for good management, and thus let communication gaps widen. The goal is to merge the professionalism of a large company with the innovation and flexibility of a small one. It's not easy.

To hold off competitors without losing market share requires use of both regular and unorthodox techniques.

Regular techniques are the solid principles of running a business. These include proper accounting practices and controls; adherence to local, state, and federal tax and labor laws; codified hiring, promotion, and dismissal guidelines; a company policy manual; standard management techniques, including engineering and project management; classic marketing approaches; and so on.

Unorthodox techniques are the innovative efforts that give you an edge. These can include: company organization; work environment; compensation incentives; creative market strategy; product architecture; development techniques and tools; and so on.

Regular techniques will help prevent failure, but unorthodox techniques are needed to achieve success.

Many start-ups fail, or at least stumble, because they don't pay attention to regular techniques. This happens for any number of reasons: lack of experience or understanding, the casual nature of a small company, time pressures to raise money and/or complete development, and so on. But a failure to attend to these issues can cause serious financial, legal, and organizational problems down the road. Companies of all sizes can have problems with the regular techniques of engineering and project management, marketing, and other product-related issues; this is where many larger companies fail, even when they're handling the other details correctly.

In a similar fashion, it's the small companies, especially start-ups, which are most likely to adopt unorthodox techniques. This is because of the lack of bureaucracy and politics; there is lower risk and higher potential rewards for doing things differently. In larger companies, management tends to resist or squash unorthodox techniques out of fear of losing control if things do work, or of looking bad if they don't. There's also the management mindset that says, "If I let this group do this, then soon other groups will want to do things other ways, and everything will be chaotic." That is precisely why innovation has a hard time thriving in large organizations.

Of course, most (though certainly not all) companies beyond a certain size handle the regular techniques well, so it's precisely the unorthodox techniques that become the differentiation, the edge your company has over your rivals.

If you're able to encourage and exploit unorthodox techniques, you'll find you have a constant source of ideas, tactics, and products.

Regular techniques strengthen the company's infrastructure, but they also make you more predictable and tend to discourage creativity. It is the unorthodox techniques that break up old ways of thinking and that stimulate new thoughts and new efforts, giving you new insights into what customers might buy and offering an edge on the competition.

In competition, there are only the regular techniques and the unorthodox techniques; still, there are many, many different ways of applying them.

The regular techniques are well-known and have largely withstood the test of time. The unorthodox techniques come and go and are often heralded as the Next Great Idea, getting on the cover of *Business Week*, *Upside*, or even *BYTE*. These include concepts such as just-in-time manufacturing, total quality management, object-oriented development, virtual corporations, horizontal corporations, and so on. Those concepts that prove successful slowly become regular techniques; the others are left behind.

When it comes right down to it, though, there are only so many approaches to running a business, developing a product, and marketing it to customers. What varies is the combination of factors, and what is rare is the ability to select the right approach for a given situation.

When rushing water is able to tumble boulders, it is because of momentum. When a diving hawk kills its prey with one blow, it is because of precise timing.

Momentum and timing are tremendous assets that exist independently of one another (though they enhance one another).

Momentum refers to the resources, weight, power, influence and so on that a given company can bring to bear. Large companies naturally have those resources in abundance, though they often have a hard time building momentum, and they can dissipate it with a single misstep: IBM lost the home market forever when it came out with the infamous IBM PCjr back in the mid-80s.

Smaller companies can bring a lot of momentum to a given market by focusing and coordinating what resources they do have, and they're often more nimble at it. But they can usually only do so when the field is clear. Note that small companies and start-ups have been the leaders in the

Internet/Web market, and that the large technology companies (Microsoft, IBM, Apple, Novell, etc.) have largely been caught flat-footed.

Timing means just that: coming out with the right product for the right price at the right time. Many of the major product success stories were founded on excellent—if sometimes inadvertent—timing. MS-DOS, Turbo Pascal, WordPerfect, and Netscape are all prime examples.

You need to build momentum in the company and its products, and then release it with precision. Building the momentum is like cranking up a crossbow; releasing it is like pulling the trigger.

It is a tremendous challenge to get all the divisions of a company to work in synchronization; all too often, they work at cross-purposes. This is particularly true with large companies, but even small ones can be riven with conflicts, strong egos, politics, and turf protection. The CEO's job is to eliminate friction, promote coordination, build enthusiasm, and release the right product at the right moment aimed in the right direction.

The release may appear to be chaotic, but it is actually well planned; the company may appear to be lurching about, but its product doesn't fail.

Organization permits the company to feign confusion; pent-up momentum permits it to feign uncertainty; careful market positioning permits it to feign weakness.

The idea: confuse the competition and make them underestimate you. Only by having excellent control over these factors can you successfully appear weak long enough to fool the competition and beat them in the marketplace.

The challenge, of course, is to do this without leaving the same impression on your customers, your partners, your resellers, and the industry in general.

To manipulate competitors, set up a situation into which the competitor is drawn, bait the trap with apparent gains, wait to apply pent-up momentum with precision.

Since success is usually achieved by lack of direct competition, the highest form of manipulation is to keep your competitors out of your intended market.

The next highest form is to lure them into a particular product position, then counter with a different position against which they cannot successfully compete. This is a bit like tennis: keep drawing your opponent to one side of the court, and the moment he or she overcommits, smash the ball back to the far side.

Set up the conditions of success for the company, rather than expecting the employees to do it on their own. Use the employees according to their individual talents and skills.

Contrary to expectations, you don't achieve success by bringing a lot of good people together, giving them a good idea, then standing back. It takes tremendous skill on the part of the CEO to create and maintain the conditions that lead to success. There are various forces that will seek to block that success; your job is to identify them and use the regular and unorthodox techniques to overcome them.

Using your employees is like rolling rocks down a slope. If the rocks are square, or if the ground is level, then the rocks stay still. If the rocks are round, and the ground is steep and high, then the rocks move with tremendous force. This is momentum.

The slope of the ground represents the momentum created in the company by the CEO. The smoothness of the stones represents the skills of the managers and employees, as well as the lack of friction between them. To build momentum, you must have both factors: slope and smoothness.

Combining regular techniques with unorthodox ones, coordinating momentum with timing, appearing disorganized while following a detailed plan—these require leadership, intelligence, and effort at every level, but most critically at the top. For if the trumpet give an uncertain sound, who shall prepare himself to the battle?

Chapter 6

Matching Strengths with Weaknesses

Every firm has weaknesses and strengths, including yours and your competitors'. The goal is to match your strengths against their weaknesses, while protecting your own weaknesses from their strengths. It sounds obvious, yet all too often we fail to honestly and correctly evaluate the strengths and weaknesses on both sides.

In his sixth chapter, Sun Tzu talks about how to harass the enemy, probe for his weak spots, avoid his strong spots, and generally adapt to the ever-changing battlefield conditions.

Attacking a weak position from a strong one is like throwing a brick through a TV set.

It can be that dramatic. Orders can drop to nothing in a matter of days or even hours when a weak market approach suddenly faces a strong one. Case in point, and one that haunts me: Borland vs. Chalcedony Software. The latter firm, a small one, marketed a Prolog implementation for MS-DOS. When Borland released Turbo Prolog, I wrote up a nice review of it in the column I had in *BYTE* at that time. The VP of Marketing at Chalcedony told me later that they knew something had happened even before they saw my review: the week that issue of *BYTE* came out, incoming calls dropped off dramatically and never recovered to the levels they were before. It wasn't that Turbo Prolog was better than the one put out by Chalcedony; it wasn't. But Borland had a vastly stronger market position, and there wasn't much Chalcedony could do to counter it.

The first company to get a product into a given marketplace has time to rest and build momentum and market position; successive companies will have to release and compete while still exhausted from the development.

The first product into a given market, if successful, can entrench itself to the point of being difficult, if not impossible, to dislodge. Products that follow then compete for the #2 position.

Aspects of the first product—bus slots, menu structures, macro languages, data formats, key/switch layout, cable routes—can themselves become *de facto* standards. Successive products must then either adhere to those standards or convince customers to accept differing implementations. Even "official" standards organizations must cope with market demands; note the tension between the group developing standards for HyperText Markup Language (HTML) and the Web browser companies (such as Netscape) that define and support proprietary HTML extensions.

Also note that the whole area of "look and feel" lawsuits (such as Lotus vs. Borland) emerged as a result of one product seeking to adhere to another product's standards.

There is a downside to being the first one in, though: if you are not significantly successful, you may end up acting as the test marketing arm for the competition, who will adopt your good points and learn from your mistakes.

Therefore, force others to enter your marketplace, instead of seeking to enter theirs.

The company that defines the marketplace has an advantage over all competitors who seek to enter that marketplace: customer inertia. If that first company has a decent solution, then it will be hard for competitors to convince customers to switch; this goes back to the whole discussion of "better" in Chapter 3. Once a product gets entrenched, it becomes hard to dislodge, especially if it remains competitive. Arrogance and complacency are the greatest dangers, as demonstrated by U.S. auto makers when they first faced Japanese imports back in the 1970s.

When competitors are relaxed, harry them and wear them out.

Seek to make the competition devote resources to a constant stream of issues, so that they are constantly reacting to your efforts instead of devising and following a well thought-out strategy of their own.

When competitors are profitable, seek to undermine their sales.

Cash flow is the lifeblood of a company. When you take sales away from a competing firm, their options and opportunities become more limited, and they begin to doubt their ability to market products. Make sure this doesn't backfire, however; if you simply become engaged in a price war (such as Borland vs. Lotus vs. Microsoft), you may never recover your own profits.

When competitors are entrenched, lure them into new areas.

Entice them into developing (or acquiring) and introducing products for markets where they won't do well, or that will drain resources from their successful areas. An overextended company does poorly on all fronts, particularly where they lack expertise. You may get unexpected help from the competition's investors and inside stockholders, who may be worried about the vulnerability of a "one-product company."

Show up in new markets where they must rush to defend themselves; swiftly develop products for unexpected markets.

You can redefine the product needs and desires for a given market segment by offering a new product; likewise, you can create new markets by looking for customers unsatisfied by current solutions. In the past Sony has excelled at this, particularly in consumer electronics, with the competition always playing catch-up.

By going into untapped markets, you can do long-term development without exhausting your resources.

If nobody is currently in that market, then you don't have to rush your product(s) out the door or spend large sums of money in making yourself heard above the competition. On the other hand, there may not be a lot of money to be made, which may be precisely why the market is untapped.

It is easiest to succeed in an uncontested market: there is no one to attack, and none from which to defend.

The challenge is making sure that a real market—defined as a set of customers who have money that they would rather spend on your product than on anything else—actually exists, or will exist in a reasonable time-frame.

A skillful CEO knows how to attack where a competitor is defenseless, and how to defend so that the competitor cannot attack.

Anyone can engage in a face-to-face slug out for market share, and many (if not most) companies do just that. Skill comes in finding the competition's weak areas while protecting your own. Subtlety and secrecy are the keys; through them, you can build momentum without leaving a trace or drawing attention to yourself, and thus better control the competition's fate.

The more the competition knows or can guess about you, the better they can forestall your efforts or defend against them.

It is good to keep your plans and efforts secret; it is even better to have the competition mistakenly think they know your secrets. Loyalty among your managers and developers is a must; see Chapter 13, "Gathering

Intelligence." When that secretly built-up momentum is released into competitors' weak spots, they can't defend against you; if it's used to out-maneuver competitors, they can't keep up with you.

Have a fast-moving, well-coordinated plan for rolling out the product in such a way that the competition is caught off guard and cannot respond in a prompt, effective manner. Chrysler did this to perfection with their introduction of the minivan in the mid-80s, and the competition has never been able to fully catch up.

When you wish to compete, the competition—however well entrenched—must engage you if you attack that which they must defend.

Determine what they have to defend, as opposed to that which they can afford not to defend. By forcing the competition to engage you, you gain credibility and publicity while exerting a degree of control over the competition's planning and resources.

When you wish to avoid competition, the competition—however strong—cannot engage you if you lead them off in the wrong direction.

If you can get the competition to focus on areas where you aren't going to be, then they won't engage you directly, though they may think they're going to. Some major software firms—including WordPerfect and Lotus—claim that Microsoft continued to urge them to develop for OS/2 after Microsoft had made a secret internal decision to drop OS/2 and push Windows 3.0 instead.

If you can make the competition commit themselves while you obscure your own plans, then you can focus your efforts more precisely, while the competition must set up a broad approach.

Make them deal with as many contingencies as possible, while you concentrate on one specific plan. Only a fraction of their efforts can then directly address your actual approach.

This way, you can then pit your entire marketing effort against a small portion of the competition's. You'll have a strong advantage in that area, and the competition will be hard pressed to defend against you.

This approach lets you take away niche markets and market segments from the competition. If you do this with several niches or segments, you can start to bridge the gaps between them and establish a more general market presence.

Each area where the competition has to focus product development and positioning comes at the cost of weakness elsewhere. And if they try to cover all their bases, they'll be weak everywhere.

There are many such divisions and dichotomies. Seek to identify those which define the competition's approach, so that you can focus yourself where they are weakest—always keeping in mind that a viable market must exist wherever you go.

A CEO who knows exactly when and how a product will be marketed can sustain a long development effort. But if the timing and approach are uncertain, then marketing and engineering can't help each other, even with a short development cycle.

The ability to predict exactly when a product will ship—with a given set of features and acceptable levels of reliability and performance—is a tremendous advantage, and one that few companies have or can maintain.

Money and size do not always guarantee success.

Often money robs a company of cleverness and intensity, while size breeds hubris, ossification, and stagnation. Here are some products you may never have heard of, all from companies that were large and profitable at the time: CalcStar and InfoStar (MicroPro), Access (Microsoft—and, no, this isn't the current database product), Jazz and Modern Jazz (Lotus), the IBM PCjr, the Apple III, PlanPerfect (WordPerfect), Sprint (Borland), the Xerox Star, the DEC Rainbow, and Friday (Ashton-Tate).

On the other hand, money and size can be a tremendous advantage when used with wisdom and focus.

Success can be created: even if the competition is bigger and stronger, you can keep them from taking you on directly.

It's not easy, but it is done. Size can be used against a large company, for all the reasons listed above.

Study the competition carefully: weigh the successes and failures of their plans.

Look at their history. What have they done well? What have they done poorly? Why have they succeeded? Why have they failed? Through these factors, you can get a sense of what will work and what won't. Look for those weak areas and blind spots. Pay special attention to their decision makers (CEOs and other influential executives); a small rudder can steer a very large ship.

Cause the competition to respond, and note their actions. Seek to get them to reveal their approach, so that you can understand what their intended market is. Challenge them in several areas, seeing where they are weak and where they are strong.

Through marketing trial balloons and flexible product configurations, you can see how the competition responds to different approaches. If you can get a competitor to react, you not only gain information, you also gain a degree of control over that company.

You may also get attention from the company that you don't want, so consider your actions carefully.

As for your own plans, keep them appearing vague and without direction: the competition cannot then anticipate you or form a counter-strategy.

Make sure your plans are clear, sharp, and flexible, but keep them to yourself.

It is by careful planning that you succeed, but the public doesn't see those plans. They see what actions you've taken, but don't understand the strategy behind them.

Of course, this again raises the issue of public perception and the impact that can have on your market. Somehow you need to instill confidence in your customers (usually done via advertising and the press) without prematurely revealing your plans to the competition.

The methods and actions by which you succeed may vary widely from product to product.

This could be true for several reasons: adapting to the market; aiming at the competition's weak spots; avoiding predictability.

Marketing strategy is like water, which adapts automatically to ground it flows over, having no fixed shape. In the same way, marketing seeks to find weak points to penetrate; it adjusts to the marketplace, the customers, and the competition; it changes as conditions change.

Marketing should be in a tight feedback loop with customers, and the ultimate feedback in marketing is the money coming in. No matter how brilliant, inventive, or logical a given market strategy might be, if it's not bringing in money, it's not working. In that case, you need to adapt or die. It's as simple as that.

The CEO who can adapt to competitors' tactics brings success to the company.

The formula for success changes constantly. Many successful companies falter because they think they can repeat their success by doing more of the same, ignoring this simple fact: the technology marketplace changes completely every 12 to 24 months.

Guy Kawasaki said some years ago that competing against Microsoft felt like putting your head in a vise and tightening it, then tightening it some more. Having been in that position myself, however briefly, I concur. Your goal should be to make your competition, real and potential, feel that way about you.

Chapter 7

Positioning Your Product

Nothing is harder than positioning your product: coming up with the right combination of features, pricing, target customers, and market representation to achieve the desired (or required) revenues. Some of the greatest successes have come about seemingly by accident, while some of the greatest flops have followed tremendous effort, expense, and calculation. It is usually clear in retrospect why some products fail and others succeed, but predicting that in advance remains a challenge.

Sun Tzu spends his seventh chapter talking about tactical maneuvers: how to deploy and shift your forces before and during combat. A common theme: with the right maneuvering, the enemy may not engage at all, thinking his cause lost before he even fights. And that, as Sun Tzu said, is the height of skill: to win without combat.

Nothing is more difficult than product positioning. The entire company must be united and coordinated in this effort.

This goes beyond how a given product is developed and presented; it encompasses how the company positions itself to its customers, to the press, to the industry, and to the competition. Some of those efforts may tug against or even contradict one another, and there may well be internal disagreements and conflicts over the subject. Add to this the growing realization that markets and economies are chaotic rather than deterministic, and you're left with the realization that any product release is a roll of the dice; the best you can hope for is to load them in your favor.

The challenges in positioning an unreleased product are first, to misdirect the competition while pushing to market, and second, to find opportunities in roadblocks.

Misdirection comes in two forms. First, you want to keep your true intentions secret as long as is essential, but no longer. Second, you want to release information that influences the competition in the direction you desire.

Roadblocks are the market's way of telling you that you didn't understand the customers. This means that your positioning is most likely wrong. Listen to your customers. Learn from them. Don't keep beating your head against them; leave that to the competition.

Describe an attractive market, then entice your competition to pursue it down a long and costly development path. This way, you can start development after they do, yet get to market first. This is the strategy of misdirection.

Keynote addresses, interviews, trade shows, white papers, and the like can be used to create and promote market concepts for others to follow, while you stay on course.

Product positioning offers both opportunity and danger.

The opportunity is a chance to build and release a successful product. The danger is a chance to magnify the flaws and weaknesses of your company while facing the best of what your competition has to offer.

If you attempt development with too many people and too much planning, you will take too long to get to market.

Each person added to a project roughly doubles the number of possible communication links, especially when you consider that Person A communicating with Person B is not identical to B communicating with A. Management structure doesn't reduce the number of links; it merely introduces impedance, signal loss, error, and noise.

Planning consists of making decisions based on current information. Too often, the amount of planning done is disproportionate to the information available; in such cases, planning should halt until more information is known.

If you attempt development with too few people and not enough planning, critical tasks will go undone.

Critical tasks can go undone for several reasons: lack of someone to do them; no recognition that they need to be done; assumption that someone else is handling them; lack of resources to do them for the person assigned to them.

If you push round-the-clock development for months on end, your developers and managers will burn out or leave. Extraordinary individuals may accomplish their tasks, but the others will get done much later.

Each person has an upper limit on the number of productive hours he or she can put in each week. When that limit is exceeded regularly, no additional progress is accomplished for the extra hours worked; in some cases, less progress is made because of errors due to physical and mental exhaustion. Likewise, suspending vacation time for anything but a very short term is usually counterproductive.

Even on a mid-term, high-intensity development path, managers will be worn out, and not all the developers will finish their tasks.

Your probability of completion is higher, but there are still risks of burnout and losing key personnel.

On a short-term, high-intensity development path, most developers will be able to keep up and complete their tasks.

The implication: seek to break mid- and long-term projects into smaller chunks, with breaks in between. The trick: making that work for large projects.

A development team that does not have the right equipment, supporting benefits, and sufficient pay, will ultimately fail and disintegrate.

In the short term, zeal, pride, *esprit de corps*, and a chance to change the world can substitute for salary, benefits, and equipment, but only in the short term. Stretch things out too long, and people will lose productivity, burn out, and start leaving. The issue isn't necessarily pay *per se*; it's how serious management's commitment to the project appears to be.

If you don't understand the pitfalls of development, the channels and paths of distribution, and the barriers to customer acceptance, you cannot correctly position your company or your products.

Note the three areas: development, distribution, marketing. All three are essential; lack of understanding in any one of the three can be damaging or even fatal to a company. If you are building a new company or are running a division within an existing one, make sure you have all three bases covered.

Unless you use or hire people who understand the markets you seek to enter, you cannot take full advantage of the opportunities in those markets.

Imagine, for example, trying to develop and sell products to the Federal Government without having someone available who has prior experience in that market. That example is obvious, but there are equivalent, if more subtle, pitfalls and opportunities in all other markets. Indeed, the greatest danger is assuming that we do understand a given market (such as entertainment) when we don't.

Product development and positioning are based on stealth and misdirection. Move quickly when opportunities arise; be prepared to shift direction and reallocate resources as the situation requires.

Fast reaction and rapid development have become easier for hardware technology, yet more difficult for software and content. There are reasons for this on both sides. Hardware is general purpose, can be built from off-the-shelf components, and the user interface—wiring, levels, switches, slots, keyboard, mouse—are standard and simple. Software and other content is special purpose, has to live within and interact with an operating environment, and has to provide information in a manner sufficiently robust and complete to encompass its functionality.

When developing products, move quickly and nimbly; when developing technology, establish a broad base and grow solidly out from there.

Develop products quickly, bringing them to market as fast as possible. There are at least three reasons for this. First, you want to give the competition as little advance notice as possible. Second, the market is a moving target; a long gap between product concept and product release can result in an outdated, underpowered product. Third, a long development cycle can result in constant adjustments to product features, which in turn can extend the development cycle even further.

Develop technology broadly, making it as complete and as general as possible. Technology prematurely exposed is too quickly copied and usually improved upon by others.

The ideal: steady, broad technology development that pays for itself by a sequence of quickly developed and quickly revised products.

To penetrate different markets, divide up your personnel; to expand market penetration, share your profits.

It is hard for a given individual or group to focus on several markets simultaneously. Devote at least one person to each market or market segment in which you are seriously interested.

Share profits based on success in a given market with all those involved in achieving that success. This will encourage your marketers and developers to seek ways to find new markets.

First assess, then plan, then act.

This may seem like an obvious sequence of events, but all too often, firms (especially start-ups) do these in reverse order: they develop some technology, create a business plan for turning it into a product, then assess the marketplace to see how to sell it. Be sure you get them in the right order.

Make use of resources outside of your company to improve your efforts.

Given the tremendous financial investment in personnel and other costs, and the investments at risk, it would be foolish not to spend significantly in this area: seminars, conferences, books, journals. It would be even more foolish not to use what you and others learn from those sources. See Chapter 13, "Gathering Intelligence."

A competitor's development team can be robbed of morale; their CEO can be misled and disheartened.

Few things are more discouraging to a development team than to think that a competing product will beat them to market, particularly if it is well-designed, well-implemented, and well-marketed. Likewise, a company's CEO may reconsider or abandon a course of action based on information about current or forthcoming product plans.

Remember, though, that this sword cuts both ways. Be alert for these tactics being applied to you by your competitors.

At the start of a venture, spirits are high; in the middle, they start to wane; towards the end, the only intent is to ship and be done with the product.

This is as true for your company as for the competition. Be prepared to compensate for this in your company and to take advantage of it in competing firms. The best cure for this syndrome: shorten the product development cycle.

Avoid engaging the competition when they are full of zeal; press them when they are tired and worn out. This way, you can maintain an emotional advantage.

"Ignore" may be even better than "avoid engaging"; a fired-up competitor can gain more energy from the responses provoked from you. Likewise, when a competing firm has morale problems and internal dissension, that is the time to appear most formidable to them; it will push the development and marketing teams to collapse.

Stay focused and tight when the competition is disorganized; stay calm and steady when they are confused. This way, you can maintain a mental advantage.

There is a trend in our industry to react to the constant barrage of changes and developments. While nimbleness is a virtue, Brownian motion is not. Few markets vanish overnight, but your customers can if they lose confidence in your focus and stability.

Pick your position and make the competition come to you; let your personnel rest while the competition drives hard to catch up; conserve your resources while the competition depletes theirs. This way, you can maintain a material advantage.

Seek to make the competition expend their resources—money, time, mind share, developers—while you conserve yours.

Don't seek to compete where the competition is well organized; don't pit your small resources directly against their large ones. This way, you can maintain a positional advantage.

If you drive into a brick wall, you may damage the wall some, but you'll hurt yourself a lot more. Look for the weak spots, the gaps in the wall—or drive around it completely.

In product positioning, don't go broadly against well-entrenched or well-supported competitors.

You can go broadly against a weak competitor, and you can go with a tight focus against a strong competitor. But if you go broadly against a strong competitor, you won't get a lot for your efforts.

Don't go up against their best development efforts.

Even if you beat them to market, you may end up paving the way for them, allowing them to take advantage of the pioneering and consumer education you've done.

Beware of abandoned markets and deserted customers.

There are opportunities there, but be careful: companies don't usually leave customers and markets out of ignorance or stupidity. Be sure you understand why the markets were abandoned, lest you fall into the same problems.

Don't block the competition's retrenchment efforts. Give them a graceful exit from competing with you. Don't press too hard against a competitor who's withdrawing.

Don't give your competitor a reason to resume or continue competition. They may re-enter the market out of stubbornness and pride, and even if they don't do well, they can undermine your success.

If you understand stealth, misdirection, targeted development, and speed, you will succeed—this is the art of product positioning.

The trick is to fool the competition and not to fool yourself. Unfortunately, the reverse happens quite often: companies begin to believe their own hype and wake up only when competitors seize market share and sales plummet. Some don't even wake up then.

The last maxim does summarize correct product positioning: plan secretly; misdirect the competition; focus your development; execute quickly. This won't guarantee success—usually, too many factors outside of your control are at work—but it does maximize the chances of success.

Chapter 8

Adjusting to Market Realities

Once you get your product out in the marketplace, you will need to adjust to the realities you find there. Your product may not be accepted as well as you like. Your actual customers may be different from those you originally targeted. There may be some critical features or benefits missing. The market you aimed at may transform or disappear. And so on. Survival will depend upon recognizing these problems and reacting to them.

The eighth chapter of Suntzu pingfa talks about tactical variations and adjusting to the realities of battle. Sun Tzu notes that it is how the general adapts to the advantages and disadvantages of the moment that often determines victory or defeat.

Don't waste time establishing yourself in vulnerable markets.

It makes little sense to spend time and money to enter a market in which you cannot defend your market share. You may be lured in by apparent short-term profits, but unless you can get in quickly and then get out quickly with little cost to your reputation, it's just not worth it.

In vertical markets, establish alliances with other firms.

A *vertical market* is typically one focused on a given industry: legal, financial services, medical, government. These markets have higher needs for special features, customized applications, and integrated solutions. Leverage your technology with the experience and technology of other firms—developers, VARs, and systems integrators.

Don't seek or expect quick revenues from markets with little cash flow.

Chances are you won't make money quickly by aiming products at, say, elementary school teachers. There may be other reasons for going into such a market, but revenue isn't one of them.

Likewise, you may find yourself in markets with long sales cycles (six months to several years). Those may ultimately prove to be lucrative, but you need to be sure you can support yourself in the meantime.

When market expansion is constrained, plan your moves wisely.

Current cash flow is not enough on which to base your decisions; you need to look at how long you can sustain that cash flow. This also means you need to pay close attention to your current customer base, since you may not be able to gain many new customers.

Battle fiercely for markets essential to your existence.

This may appear obvious, but many firms, large and small, have made the mistake at one point or another of taking their core markets for granted: WordStar, Lotus, WordPerfect, Apple, IBM, AT&T, Xerox—the list goes on. A fierce defense will not only help preserve your market, it will discourage competitors and build confidence among your customers.

There are products that you shouldn't develop, companies you shouldn't challenge, customers you shouldn't win, markets you shouldn't enter, recommendations from the board of directors you shouldn't follow.

Just because you can develop a given product, compete against a given company, win customers, penetrate markets, and/or fulfill the wishes of the board of directors doesn't mean that you should. It is possible to succeed in doing these things and to damage the company in the process, or at least to divert yourself from more significant opportunities.

If you understand all these factors, you can successfully direct the company and capture market share.

> You must know what not to do, as well as what to do.

If you don't understand these factors, you won't be able to establish market position, even if you're familiar with the market.

> Knowing the market isn't enough if you don't know how to direct product development and marketing.

If you understand the factors, but you don't understand how and when to apply them, you won't be able to effectively direct the company.

> Knowing the factors isn't enough; you have to know how and when to use them. This is the difference between having knowledge and having skill in applying that knowledge.

To be effective, consider both positive and negative factors. By considering the positive factors, you construct a plan that can succeed. By considering the negative factors, you anticipate problems and avoid pitfalls.

> Both sides are essential. A CEO who looks only at positive factors will guide the company over the cliff's edge; one who looks only at the nega-

tive factors will never create the products and attitudes that are necessary for success.

Intimidate competitors by taking market and profit away from them.

When you succeed in capturing market share and cutting into the competition's profits, you discourage them and make them think twice about continuing to compete with you.

Wear out competitors by creating new problems and challenges for them.

By introducing a series of actions to which the competition must respond, you keep them off-balance and cause them to expend resources that they could otherwise use for their own plans.

Distract competitors by enticing them with possible profit.

If you can draw the competition into markets that you don't want, then they will spend resources in those markets that they would otherwise spend competing with you.

Don't rely on the competition not entering a given market; instead, have a plan for dealing with them if they do.

If you plan for them entering the market and they don't, then you have lost little. If you don't plan for it and they do, then you have lost much.

Don't count on the competition not attacking a given product; instead, make that product strong and unassailable.

If you assume that a product won't have serious competition, you won't be as thorough in making it excellent and compelling. This will make your customers dissatisfied; it will also invite the competition to supply products of its own.

There are five traits in a CEO that can lead to company failure:

If overly reckless, the CEO may lead the company into an exposed position.

Reckless means not paying attention to negative factors, assuming everything will go well for your products, and/or assuming the competition isn't as good and as smart as you.

If overly timid, the CEO may miss opportunities and lose market share.

Timid means not paying attention to the positive factors, not being willing to take risks when the rewards are significant, and not responding aggressively to competitors.

If overly proud, the CEO may be prodded into rash actions.

The technology industry is led by people with strong personalities and large egos. Many business decisions have been made out of pride or anger; any number of back issues of *Forbes*, *Fortune* and the *Wall Street Journal* will confirm that.

If overly sensitive, the CEO may be manipulated through accusations and innuendo.

Again, many significant decisions have been made because the CEO wanted to maintain or disprove a certain image, rather than for sound business reasons.

If overly compassionate, the CEO may not make the hard choices about personnel to keep the company going, and thus may endanger the jobs of all.

I'm not sure that there's a big problem in this industry with being overly compassionate; too often, the opposite is the rule. But there are cases, such as at Compaq, WordPerfect, and Kodak, of CEOs who have stepped down or been forced out because they were unwilling to make necessary payroll cuts.

Consider this: when development fails, sales and profits decline, and the CEO is replaced, it is usually because of one or more of these traits.

Make your own list of departed CEOs and see how many fell into these categories. Then ask yourself if you fit in—and where.

Here's a positive summary: know the factors given at the start of the chapter and understand how to respond to them; create plans from a position of wisdom and skill; be willing to make the hard decisions when faced with the realities of the marketplace.

Chapter 9

Leading Your Company

Whatever your title—founder, chief executive officer, president, business unit manager—it's up to you to provide leadership. That means navigating through the treacherous shoals and shifting currents of the marketplace. You have to set an intelligent, directed, yet flexible course: don't run the ship in a straight course upon the rocks, but don't tack back and forth so often that you never get anywhere.

Through all that, you have to deal with competitors who are after the same customers, the same dollars that you need to meet payroll and pay rent. You've got to know how to read their actions (or lack thereof), how to sift and interpret the thousand little bits of data that come from them in a myriad of ways.

Leadership also means setting the standards and the tone for how things are done and how people are treated within your company. The signs you use to detect problems in other companies are just as valid inside your own.

In his ninth chapter, Sun Tzu talks about how a general needs to deal with terrain, read the enemy, and govern troops. As one Chinese commentator said of a 5th century B.C. general, "His civil virtues endeared him to the people, his martial prowess kept his enemies in awe" (The Art of War, James Clavell, ed., p. 49). Not a bad model to follow.

When entering the marketplace through niche or vertical markets, don't cut yourself off from more general use of your products. Start out in a defensible niche market, and be prepared to move into horizontal markets.

A *horizontal market* is a broad one, cutting across a wide variety of organizations and groups. The word processing market is a horizontal one; word processors are used at work, school, and home.

A *vertical market* is typically one focused on a given industry: legal, financial services, medical, government. Specialized word processing systems for documents meeting government specifications is an example of a vertical market.

A *niche market* is a relatively small market oriented around a set of customer needs and interests, usually a subset of a larger horizontal or vertical market. HTML editors are an example of a niche market.

If you are using niche or vertical markets as a doorway into more general horizontal markets, make sure your technology and products are readily adaptable to broader uses. Aim for a market where you know you can get adoption, and use that as the foundation for spreading into more general use.

This concept is discussed in greater detail in *Crossing the Chasm* by Geoffrey Moore. He talks about the challenges of spreading out to mainstream customers after having established a beachhead among early adopters. Read the book.

Be wary of going from a horizontal market into niche or vertical markets occupied by competitors.

Trying to move a general product into a niche market already occupied by competing specialized products may be a waste of resources. Besides dealing with the problems of customer loyalty and legacy requirements, you'll also find that your general product can't provide the special features of the niche products, and that you can't keep up with the speed of product revision of your competitors. Example: general word processors trying to compete with dedicated HTML editors.

In short, you may be able to do it, but the return on investment is low at best, and it may be more trouble than it's worth.

You have a better chance for adapting a general product for a vertical market, especially if the customers there are interested in compatibility with horizontal markets. Again, the key is whether there are competitors already established.

The worst case is if there are established competitors who have a general product. Classic example: WordPerfect has dominated the legal market for some time, and other word processing companies seeking to penetrate that market have found it very tough to do so.

Don't drag out a product introduction: move into post-release distribution, press contacts, and advertising as quickly as possible.

There are few things worse than introducing a new product and not having it be readily available to customers. This is an error that Apple has made on several occasions, failing to anticipate product demand and creating both a huge backlog and a lot of frustrated customers. Be prepared to move product quickly into channels and to get it into the hands of customers immediately after ship.

As important is an intense, broad, and coordinated effort to get your product in front of the press. I find it amazing (not to mention short-sighted and stupid) that companies that will spend tens or even hundreds of thousands of dollars on advertising suddenly turn cheap and uncooperative when it comes to providing review products to press contacts.

Finally, advertising should be coordinated with product release. Many companies forgo advertising, citing oft-quoted (but seldom documented) studies saying that word-of-mouth is the primary reason customers select or consider a given product. I suspect that's true, but it overlooks one little fact: people don't talk or ask about products they don't know about. Distributors and resellers are the same way. Advertising builds word of mouth; without it, people don't know about your product, or they doubt your financial underpinnings.

Don't attack a competing product before it is released: attack instead just as the product is released, but before it becomes established.

This point can be argued, given the long times between announcement and release that have become common in the industry. Even so, the drawbacks to attacking an unreleased product are several. First, you draw attention to that product, giving the product credibility even though it doesn't yet exist. Thus, if you mention it at all, it should only be to point out that it doesn't yet exist. Second, you give the product's company a chance to reposition the product—or even to modify it—so that they can discredit or deflect your attack. Third, you may appear to the market and the industry to be desperate—that you are afraid of a product that hasn't even shipped.

It is better to wait until the competition has committed itself, both in terms of the product and the markets targeted, then to go after the product while it's still unestablished. That is the point at which the product and its company are most vulnerable.

The exception to this rule: if the competition is pre-announcing products in order to freeze customer decisions, then you should aggressively attack them for offering nothing at all. This is the classic "We're shipping; they're not" approach.

Be careful about attacking a competing product when the competition is desperate and has no fallback position.

Sun Tzu cautions against attacking an army with a river at its back; likewise, you need to be careful about backing the competition into a corner. In such cases, they will have nothing to lose and may take steps that will damage you, such as starting a price war.

Start out your product at a higher price, then lower the price as necessary; do not come out at a lower price, then expect to be able to raise the price.

Once a retail price has been set, it is difficult to raise it without hurting sales significantly. It is much easier to have a higher retail price initially, then lower it (or at least lower the distributor price) as time goes on.

Some markets (such as computer software) allow and, to an extent, demand a low "introductory" price. This is sometimes masked as an "upgrade" price, good for a specific period of time. This is one of the few cases in which you can later raise your price, but even this is becoming increasingly difficult.

The latest trend is to have no standard retail price (SRP) at all. That way, you can in theory be as flexible as you want to be. The end result will be even greater downward price pressure.

When trying to create a new product category, don't position yourself as competing with or replacing other products. Instead, focus on building the market as quickly as possible. If other firms attempt to compete with you, have a plan to redefine your product category so that you can put distance between your product and theirs.

Creating a new product category is difficult enough; the last thing you want to do is directly take on existing products, which, by definition, lie in other categories. Don't try to replace those products; instead, position yourself as complementing them or as performing a significant task that they don't handle well. There are two key reasons for this. First, you don't want the customers to think that they are choosing between you and an existing product; if they think that, then you are failing to establish a new product category. Second, you don't want to attract the attention of the competition; you have enough to worry about.

As noted, if either the customers or other companies see you as competition, be prepared to redefine the product category to diminish that. Eventually, you will want to expand the market for your competition, but you need to get established first.

As you move into a horizontal market, focus on getting the best market position available. Keep some niche or vertical markets as a fallback position, in case your competitors pressure or overwhelm you.

All fairly straightforward: keep a good foundation while expanding your market. This is especially important because your cash flow almost certainly won't ramp up as fast as you'd like, even if sales do.

When you discover an unoccupied niche market, position yourself to block competitors and to gain revenues from it that will help your efforts elsewhere.

With all the companies out there scrambling for profits, it's hard to believe that there are still untapped markets. There are, though—they come into being as business, society, technology, and the economy change. But they tend to be found and filled quickly, so if you discover one, you need to move fast.

When economic, market, or other factors threaten to make product release difficult or expensive, wait if possible until conditions are more favorable.

Depending upon the product and its intended market, there may be various reasons to delay release: waiting for a better time of year, synchronizing with supporting software or hardware, letting the competition make the first move, synchronizing with press and trade show exposure, not enough money for advertising, and so on.

If this is your first or only product, your options may be more limited. You may have to launch anyway and hope for the best. You may have to scale down the company size and burn rate until better conditions appear. You may have to do both. Or you may have to find more money, a partner, or someone interested in acquisition—but, as noted in Chapter 1, this is the worst circumstance under which to raise money or sell out.

Beware of niche markets that offer little return, that have little in common with horizontal markets, or that have significant development or support requirements.

Any one of these three factors—low return on investment, low technology leverage, high development or support requirements—is enough to make a given niche market a waste of resources. Value-added resellers (VARs) can often handle these markets better than can actual product companies.

Seek to entice the competition into such markets, then position yourself between them and the broader markets.

Let others spend their resources on those markets, while you better establish your position in the general market.

Be careful when expanding into markets that you don't understand or with which you have little experience, lest you give away your plans or sales to more experienced competitors without gaining much.

You may have products, technology, or services well-suited to the market, but if you don't understand the market itself, you could lose whatever advantage you have while giving great ideas to the competition.

When you are encroaching upon the competition's market, yet they make little visible response, it is because they are very confident. Be careful.

It is possible, of course, that they're overconfident or even just stupid, but it still pays to be cautious. They almost certainly know some things you don't, even if they aren't taking full advantage of them.

When they try to pick a fight without directly competing, it's because they want you to make the first move.

Don't let the competition taunt you into showing your plans too soon. This can be a hard choice: if the competition raises questions about you in the minds of your potential customers or in the industry press, you may have to respond somehow. In that case, you have to balance customer and press relations with the need not to lay out your plans too far ahead of time.

When the market seems too easy to get into, it may be a trap.

There ain't no such thing as a free lunch. If things are going too well, start asking yourself why no one else has done this up until now. You may have found a pot of gold, but there aren't many of those; what you may have instead is a tar pit, easy to get into, but hard to get out of.

When customers start delaying or reconsidering evaluations, it's because the competition is advancing.

It's a danger signal when your customers' sales cycles keep dragging out; it means that they are seriously considering alternative solutions. If it's because you've made serious errors, then it's simply your fault. But if your product is still strong, then the competition must be making inroads somehow, either publicly or privately.

When the competition increases security, it's because they want to misdirect you.

When sources within the company become quiet, then treat with suspicion the information that does come out.

Press leaks and articles mean the competition is getting ready to release products. A sudden flurry of press releases means product ship is imminent.

There are dozens of publications and scores of journalists who need articles to write. They will publish the information they can get, much of which comes straight from the companies in question; the frequency and prominence of the articles usually corresponds to the imminence of product release. Once the PR agencies start cranking out the press releases, you know that the product is about to ship.

When rumors are detailed, then you know that the competition's product development is proceeding quickly; when they are vague, then you know that the competition is focusing on general technology.

Technology may be exciting, but details only come as that technology is implemented in products that work. The more detailed the rumors, the more concrete the product.

When developers within the competition change assignments, you know that a new project is starting; when explicit recruiting ads appear in the paper, you know that the project has gained acceptance.

Internal transfers to new projects almost always come first; indeed, many new products start as part-time "skunk works" projects by current employees, usually the best developers. Many such projects die without ever seeing the light of day, so as long as there is no external notice about it, don't be too concerned.

The key is when help-wanted ads start appearing, asking for engineers and other development types to work on the new technology. At that point, you know the project is serious: both because the competition is willing to spend money to hire new people (no light decision) and because they are willing to publicize the effort. Of course, it may be a misdirection ploy.

When your competition speaks modestly while continuing full-scale development, they may be getting ready to enter the market aggressively.

Pay attention when the competition downplays their plans in a given area while continuing to spend resources heavily. They wish to lull everyone else while preparing to make a major move.

Blustering words and the appearance of a strong marketing effort may mask an effort to withdraw from a given market segment or to cover up significant problems.

Many companies get the most vocal when they have the most to hide. That's because they don't want to jeopardize what sales efforts they have going on, and they don't want to start a domino effect.

Those who praise your products are seeking a rest from competition.

They may want the customers to see your products and theirs as being complementary; they may be signaling that they want to talk with you; they may be trying to reposition their products into new markets and/or out of current ones.

Those who talk about strategic alliances without showing good faith are up to no good.

Quick, name three "strategic alliances" in the technology industry that have worked out well for all parties involved. For that matter, name one.

When the competition starts comparing their products against various aspects of yours, they are preparing for direct competition.

The real clue is when the competition mentions you or your products in their ads, on their packaging, or in comments to the press.

When they quickly move a major product into a new market, they expect supporting products to follow shortly.

Few major products or services can stand alone in a new market. They need various supporting products and services, often from other firms. A company making a fast push into a new market either has supporting products and services lined up, or it is in for a rude awakening.

When they release tentative information on products and positioning, they are attempting to lure you into revealing your own plans.

When the competition starts speculating on their future developments, they may be trying to get you to respond, hoping you'll expose some of your own plans.

When the competition's employees cut back on personal spending, they are concerned about future paychecks.

When employees start putting off purchases and delaying repairs, then they have questions about the company's viability. This applies to your own company as well as to the competition.

When those sent out on field research ask quietly about jobs elsewhere, they are concerned about their current positions.

If employees are sounding out the job market, they have reasons to leave the company: pay, opportunity, stability, future.

When the company fails to make simple enhancements that can win them new customers, it is getting low on resources.

They may not have the capital to expand; they may not have the development and marketing resources; or they may just be too consumed with their current markets.

When consultants and VARs start making money in a given market segment, it is because your competition is withdrawing from that segment.

Consultants and VARs usually step in to help customers convert legacy files and shrinkwrap applications over to support new replacement applications, which may be custom or commercial. For example, an entire industry arose for a while to help convert Wang word processor files to WordStar, WordPerfect, or whatever other format was needed.

When there are negative leaks about the competition in the press, it means that employees there are unhappy with company direction.

Happy employees seldom leak unfavorable information to the press, but beware of unhappy ones, particularly developers and engineers. As Robert

X. Cringely has noted, they are the ones most likely to be unhappy with management policy and direction, and the ones most likely to let columnists like Cringely know. The advent of anonymous mail routers on the Internet makes this a safe form of expression.

When internal disputes become public, it means the CEO's authority is weakening.

The more visible the power plays and arguments within a company, the less control and authority the CEO has or is able to exercise effectively.

When there is constant reorganization, the company is in disarray.

Reorganization means that the company structure does not function properly for the problems facing it. Constant reorganization means that no one knows how to solve the problems facing the company. Consider Apple, which seems to have been reorganizing itself annually (at least) for the last decade.

When company officials show anger or frustration in public, they are becoming exhausted.

Public composure is a good test of emotional strength and security. When internal and external challenges become overwhelming, that composure starts to slip during public appearances, especially press conferences and question-and-answer (Q&A) sessions.

When they splurge on advertising and promotions, hand out bonuses, cut margins, and stop supporting older products, they are desperate.

The company recognizes that it's in trouble, and it's taking various extreme measures to hold onto employees, to win (or keep) customers, and to turn things around.

When there are internal rumors, hallway whisperings, and lackluster efforts, it means the employees have lost confidence in the CEO.

When employees have confidence in the CEO, then they can bear up under stress and adversity, and they focus on what advances the company. When they lack confidence in the CEO's ability to lead and manage the company, then everything seems difficult, and they focus on their own needs and wants.

Large bonuses and perks among the rank and file indicate that the company leaders are having a hard time keeping employees and getting projects completed.

As managers and developers start to leave, those left behind get offered large sums and nice benefits to entice them to stay. This is especially true when a project is in serious trouble and those working on it have become discouraged.

Firings and demotions mean that discipline has been lax and employees no longer follow the leaders.

These moves indicate either a failure to achieve or an unwillingness to follow.

If company leaders are harsh at first, then later try to appease or win the favor of the employees, they've taken the worst possible approach.

By such a course, you will get neither discipline nor enthusiasm; employees will distrust and disrespect you.

When the competition's morale is high, yet they neither move against you nor withdraw from the market, find out what's going on.

They know something significant is about to happen, but they don't want you to know about it—therefore, you must find out.

The key is to focus your resources, watch your competitors carefully, and hire the right people.

Given, of course, that you have a product that can succeed.

The person who makes no plans and ignores competitors will be pushed out of the market by them.

Even a small company can win out over a large one if the large company is overconfident; the danger is greater when the companies are closer in size.

Your developers prefer product quality over shoddiness, and product recognition to obscurity. Seek for product excellence and you will keep your developers happy and productive, helping you to achieve success.

Developers want to have pride in what they produce, and that is best satisfied by a visible, successful product of high quality. When developers are asked to deliberately cut corners on quality, they start to look for work elsewhere.

If you push employees hard without first gaining their support, they won't deliver what you ask.

They will find ways—consciously and unconsciously—to undermine your efforts, and they will try to either drive you out or leave when they have a better opportunity. In any case, they will tend to follow their own goals, instead of working with you on shared goals.

If you fail to make your employees accountable after gaining their support, they won't deliver what you need.

Support is not enough; they must realize that they will be held responsible for achieving what is necessary. That which gets measured, gets accomplished.

Thus, you must first gain loyalty, then you must hold your employees accountable for what the company requires; this way you can succeed.

This is the proper order, because if they are loyal and supportive, they will want to be accountable and therefore will put forth the effort to achieve.

If wise policies and directives are consistently enforced, employees will be satisfied.

Two key words here: "wise" and "consistent." For some unfathomable reason, CEOs and senior managers often lose sight of the fact that they are dealing with grown-ups who will immediately recognize foolish or arbitrary policies. At best, you will lose their respect and confidence; at worst, you will lose them to the competition.

Leadership must be both internal and external. You must place equal value on internal direction and external strategy. Neglecting one will open the door for failure, no matter how well you perform on the other.

Chapter 10

Dealing with Obstacles

Problems will arise, both inside and outside the company. Those outside have to do with the customers: what their demands and expectations are. Those inside have to do with the employees: their commitment, their competency, and their interactions with each other. Both are ultimately the responsibility of the CEO. A good CEO cannot guarantee success, because of the vagaries of the marketplace. However, a bad CEO almost always brings about poor sales and internal turmoil.

Sun Tzu talks in his tenth chapter about various types of terrain and how to deal with them, and about various problems within the ranks and how they came about. His conclusion: if you know the enemy and know yourself, then your victory is not at risk.

There are six kinds of markets: open, entrapping, indecisive, narrow, custom, and future.

The first part of this chapter deals with six general classes of markets. These markets are defined in terms of how large they are, what kind of sales opportunities are in them, and what it will take to get money out of them. Your challenge is correctly recognizing the nature(s) of the market you've entered.

An open market is one that you and any number of competitors can readily enter. The first company to win acceptance among customers and to establish its attributes as standards has a powerful advantage.

Case in point: the desktop graphical user interface market was open for a long time, until Microsoft finally won it with Windows 3.0. That was not a foregone victory, though, given the negative response to and lackluster sales of Windows 2.0 and Windows 386. If GeoWorks had come out with PC/GEOS a year or two earlier, or if Apple had licensed the Macintosh OS to hardware manufacturers several years sooner, the market might be quite different now.

In much the same way, the current race to provide high-bandwidth services to mass consumer and business markets—the so-called information superhighway—is under way. The race may not have a single winner, but the company or companies that get there first will have a tremendous advantage over those who lag behind.

An entrapping market is one that you can enter only by making commitments that will require long-term support. If the competition isn't prepared to face you, then you can succeed in this market; if they are, then you may fail to gain the benefits of the market, yet be stuck with ongoing support costs.

Certain niche and vertical markets can be entrapping, particularly where you have large sales to a small number of customers. Many government markets are like this, since in order to win a contract you may have to guarantee support for your product over a number of years.

The potential nightmare here is finding yourself having to support a customer base due to long-term contracts, yet making little money on it or, worse yet, losing money. Think carefully before entering such a market, and watch what you sign.

An indecisive market is one that holds no clear advantage for you or the competition. The key is to lure the competition into the market, then to go focus on a better market elsewhere.

Getting the competition to fill that market for you has two advantages. First, it gives you a reason not to be in there yourself. Second, it consumes the competition's resources without yielding much of a payoff.

A narrow market is one that is really only big enough to support one company in your product area. You need to capture this market first, then defend it from the competition. If the competition is already in the market, do not enter and compete with them unless they are not yet established.

There are product niches that, once filled, are not worth competing for. If you can get in first with a solid product, then you can probably capture and hold most of the potential market share. If someone else has done it first, then it's probably not worth the effort unless (a) their product is significantly lacking or (b) you can expand the overall market size.

A custom market requires extra development and support efforts to win customers. You must capture that market first, or else it won't be worth the resources spent on it. If the competition is already in it, seek another market.

Custom markets are like narrow markets, but much smaller; each customer is, in essence, a separate market, and extra development is almost always required. It is difficult to take existing customers away from the competition in a custom market, even where there is significant dissatisfaction. It is, however, possible to learn from the competition and to use that to capture new customers.

The biggest danger in this market: charging too little for your product and services. If you do that, it'll bleed you to death.

A future market exists only in potential and will not yield customers for some time to come. All companies are at an equal disadvantage, and it is difficult to engage in competition in such a market.

Future markets present a danger and an opportunity. The opportunity is that future markets at some point become open or narrow markets, and the first company in has a real advantage. The danger is that going into a future market too soon or with the wrong product won't yield much in sales and will give away to the competition both product ideas and market research. This is why it is often the second or third product shipping that ends up dominating that market.

These are the principles relating to these six kinds of markets. Understand them and study them with great care.

Certain characteristics and attributes determine the "landscape" of a given market. You need to be both able and willing to look honestly at those characteristics and to draw the appropriate conclusions. If you misread the market, out of ignorance or wishful thinking, you will bring failure upon yourself and your company.

Some company problems are not a natural consequence of doing business, but are the responsibility of the CEO. These problems include: market rout, insubordination, product failure, internal conflict, organizational collapse, and mismanagement.

An earlier chapter stated that the CEO is responsible for the company's strength. These problems are symptoms of various failures on the part of the CEO in that responsibility. When you see these problems in the competition or—Heaven forbid—in your own company, you know where the problem lies.

All other things being equal, if a company takes on a competitor with much greater resources, the result is a market rout.

If the other company has greater resources and has products, developers, and marketers as good as yours, you'll get your head handed to you. Case in point: no sane person would introduce a new Windows-based word processor to go up against Microsoft Word for Windows. Anyone foolish enough to do this has ignored all the advice in Chapter 3, and there's no one else to blame.

When developers are bright and confident, but the managers are of poor quality, the result is insubordination.

It is foolish and wasteful to hire outstanding developers and engineers, then to hire mediocre (or worse) managers. The developers will have no respect for the managers and will disobey or subvert their directives.

When managers are bright and confident, but the developers are of poor quality, the result is product failure.

Even the best managers can't get blood from a turnip. The "warm bodies" approach to development will always fail in the long run, and usually fails in the short run. Products will be late, if they ever ship at all, and they will fall short of what is needed.

When senior managers are angry and insubordinate and push ahead their projects and products without a company-wide strategy or the approval of the CEO, the result is internal conflict.

This problem can show up in one of two ways. First, the senior manager is more interested in empire-building and self-advancement than in serving the good of the company and its employees, and so pushes a given project ahead to that end. Second, the senior manager realizes the company is headed down the wrong direction, but can't get the CEO to listen, and so pushes ahead with a given project to help save the company.

In either case, the CEO is at fault for not leading the company properly and for not listening to the senior managers carefully.

When the CEO lacks influence and skill, when assignments and responsibilities are unclear, and when there is not clear delegation of responsibility and the commensurate authority, the result is organizational collapse.

The CEO is responsible for the organization of the entire company. To accomplish this effectively, the CEO must set an example for the rest of the company, must establish priorities and responsibilities among the senior managers, and must delegate authority commensurate with those assignments.

This last point—delegation of authority—is critical. Without it, the company becomes inefficient, employee morale suffers, and the CEO will lose senior managers and other employees.

When the CEO is unable to assess the competition and allows an inferior product to be placed in competition against a superior one, attempts to use poor developers to compete against good ones, or fails to put the best people in the key positions, the result is mismanagement.

Again, the CEO is responsible for seeing that the company is using the best resources possible to compete against other companies. This may seem obvious, but the mistakes above are made quite often throughout the technology industry.

These are six paths to failure. You need to be aware of these and to look for them within your company.

You should regularly check for these problems, and then take active steps to solve them.

The nature of a given market can be a help to the company; however, you must also be able to size up the competition and to correctly judge the time to market, the sales potential, and the difficulty of market penetration in order to assure success. If you bring products to market knowing these factors, you'll probably succeed; if you don't know these factors, you'll probably fail.

It's not enough to know the market itself. You need to be able to estimate how both your company and the competition will do in that market. As always, intellectual honesty is a must, and self-deception or wishful thinking will only hurt your firm.

If a market opportunity is sure to bring success, to increase profits, and to ensure the survival of the company, you must enter that market, even if the directors disagree.

There is, of course, a large risk in pushing into a market against the wishes of the directors, but that's why CEOs get the salaries and perks that they do.

On the other hand, if it's sure to bring failure, to lose money, or to endanger the company, you must not enter that market, even though the directors insist on it.

Likewise, the CEO needs to know what risks not to take, even if the board thinks otherwise. This, too, involves risk—but it is better to be fired than to lead the company into disaster. Unfortunately, it appears that some CEOs don't believe that.

The CEO who pushes a new product forward without seeking all the glory, and who withdraws from a market without worrying about criticism or blame, but whose sole purpose is to protect employees and to serve the best interests of the company and its investors, is rare and priceless.

This approach will win tremendous loyalty from employees and will draw forth their finest efforts. At the same time, the company will be well served, with the CEO putting the company's well-being ahead of ego or self-protection.

If you look upon your employees with a sense of personal responsibility, they will stay with the company even through difficult times. If you treat each one as an important individual, they will give all they have to help the company succeed.

All management books aside, there are few things as powerful as personal loyalty—and that only comes when you give the employees reason to trust and respect you, and when they know that you trust and respect them. Loyalty, after all, is a two-way street.

If you are too indulgent to demand accountability, too friendly to enforce authority, and too casual to require organization, then your employees will be like spoiled children and will be useless.

To build trust and respect among the employees, you must treat them like professionals, not like friends or relatives, and you must expect them to behave like professionals. This is not necessarily the same as "behaving in a professional manner," which is often an excuse for officiousness and high control needs, such as strict dress codes, rigid working hours, and other signs of insecurity.

If you know that you can bring your product to market, but you don't know if the competition is vulnerable, you're only halfway to victory.

Point one: you need to know that you can sell against the competition.

If you know the competition is vulnerable, but you don't know if you can bring your product to market, you're only halfway to victory.

Point two: you need to know that you can develop and ship the appropriate product in a timely fashion.

If you know the competition is vulnerable and that you can bring your product to market, but you don't know if the marketplace is one you can succeed in, you're only halfway to victory.

Point three: you need to know that customers will spend their money on your product rather than on something else.

Thus, those who are experts at competing don't get distracted once their efforts are set in motion, nor do they lose focus when competition is begun.

You need focus and endurance while developing; you need energy and persistence when marketing.

If you understand your own company and your competitors, success will never be in danger. If you understand the market and the economy as well, success will be complete.

You are unlikely to fail if you know what your company is capable of creating and marketing, and if you know the same of the competition. But that's not enough for complete success: for that, you need to know what the customers will buy.

It is important to recognize how different market situations can arise and why each requires its own response. If we've solved an earlier crisis a given way, we may be tempted to use the same approach for successive problems, whether or not that solution is appropriate. It is also important to realize that internal problems are as critical—and require as much thought and effort—as external ones.

Chapter 11

Reacting to Market Situations

The test of leadership is to deal with events that are thrust upon you, as well as those which you or those under your stewardship have brought about. You must recognize each situation, evaluate it honestly, and handle it appropriately. Of course, you'll have to do all that while still dealing with your employees, your customers, and the competition. But no one ever said this would be easy.

Sun Tzu, in Chapter 11, talks about the nine tactical situations that a general may have to deal with, and the corresponding demands for both internal leadership and external conflict. But he sums up the chapter, and perhaps the whole book, with a single comment: "To gather his army and lead it into danger—that is the duty of the general."

In competing for a market segment, there are nine situations in which you may find yourself: stalemated; tentative; critical; cooperative; vital; ascendant; difficult; trapped; desperate.

These names are shorthand for various market conditions you may face within a given market segment (or perhaps in your entire market). Each situation is defined by the degree of market penetration, the business opportunities, the requirements and demands of the customers, and the present and potential competition.

When you and the competition trade attacks from the safety of your respective segments, the situation is stalemated. Don't worry about the competition; instead, focus on how well your company is functioning internally.

In this situation, neither company is making a dent in the other's market. There is no real threat, but there is no real growth, either.

Don't waste resources on the competition, because you and they don't have the same market base. Spend your resources on your products and on your customers. There is no immediate threat, so concentrate on getting the company moving toward a common goal.

Companies tend to be unified when facing great challenges, but there's a risk of internal disputes before commitments have been made.

When the company is deep into a given commitment or faces serious outside challenges, the employees and managers tend to pull together. But when the commitment has not been made and the risk is not yet there, there can be a lot of disagreement about what to do and how to do it.

All the divisions in your company should be able to work together. You may wonder, "Can marketing, engineering, and administration really work together?" Yes, they can. After all, many bitter marketplace rivals have joined forces when threatened by a common foe.

In other words, if competing firms can set aside differences for the sake of mutual profit and survival, then surely groups within the same company can do the same.

Different divisions and individuals can then be focused on key tasks as the market situation requires.

With universal commitment and the ability to work together, the company can bear down and solve problems.

This is the essence of management: to have a uniform level of commitment from the CEO down to the humblest employee.

Two points. First, there must be a sufficient (if not superlative) level of commitment. Second, it must exceed some given standard at all levels. Too little commitment at any level can lead to cynicism, frustration, and burnout on the other levels.

When you have lightly penetrated the competition's segment, the situation is tentative. Don't slow down your marketing efforts; focus on communication within the company.

When you first start to take customers away from the competition, you are most vulnerable to a strong response from them, particularly using the criticism of your product as being nonstandard ("Everyone else uses our product; why take a risk on theirs?").

To deal with this, press ahead rapidly, gaining customers and market share as fast as possible. The competition is going to respond at some point, and you need to have as large a base as possible. This can become a risky situation very quickly; the different divisions need to communicate and coordinate well in order to continue to gain market share.

Take advantage of the competition's blind spots, enter the market by ways they don't expect, penetrate areas where they are weak.

In other words, be unpredictable. Also expect the competition to attempt all these efforts against you.

Appear tentative at first, so that the competition will underestimate you; then move rapidly and surely so that they cannot keep up with you.

Few things are better than to have the competition think little of you. It leads them into complacency and disdain; they will cease to pay attention to you, and they will be unprepared to respond to your actions.

When the market segment can give significant advantage to you or to the competition, the situation is critical. Don't worry about engaging the competition; instead, bring all your resources to bear to capture the segment as quickly as possible.

The first one there has a significant advantage over the other and will be very difficult to dislodge.

If the competition got there first, don't waste resources trying to dislodge them; it probably won't work. If you got there first, don't waste resources attacking the competition; it isn't necessary. Either you or the competition will gain that key segment, so focus on securing it as quickly and completely as possible.

The deeper and more successfully you cut into the competition's market share, the greater your company morale and enthusiasm, and the harder you are to overcome.

Success breeds success. It also breeds excitement, confidence, and fun. You will keep your existing personnel and attract excellent ones from outside the company. With luck, it will have the opposite effect on the competition, causing discouragement and defections.

When the market segment can be readily shared by several firms, the situation is cooperative. Don't leave openings in your market approach; focus on your weak spots.

There are some markets where multiple products, or multiple sources for a given product, are desirable or even required, such as microprocessors. Or the situation may demand that products from different companies work well with each other; witness the ongoing cooperation, sometimes grudging, in the marketplace for Internet/Web software. In these cases, cooperation becomes essential.

Fill every nook and cranny of this market that you can; otherwise, the competition may do so and slowly force you out. Look for areas where the competition might leverage itself and push you out of the segment a bit more.

When the market segment opens the door into several other segments, the situation is vital. Branch out quickly into those segments, but first do customer research and premarketing in each.

There are both direct and indirect versions of this situation. In the direct version, capturing a key segment gives you a tremendous advantage in moving into other segments. This is what Microsoft accomplished by winning the desktop GUI segment, and Microsoft has leveraged that position highly in productivity application software.

In the indirect version, capturing a key segment gives you a "back door" opportunity to move into other segments. This is the "Trojan Horse" strategy, and it allowed Apple (via desktop publishing) to move the Macintosh into Fortune 500 companies in a way they would never have been able to do otherwise.

When you capture such a segment, use it to move quickly into the other connected segments, even while securing your position in the vital segment. But first talk with customers in connected segments to get product feedback and to secure cooperation in selling to them. Don't assume that the approach that worked in this segment will work in the connected ones.

When you have made significant inroads in the competition's segment and have won over important customer accounts, the situation is ascendant. Aggressively seize market share; make sure you have devoted all the resources necessary to do so.

This represents successful capture of market share from the competition.

Capture all the market share and customers you can and milk the situation for all that it's worth, both to gain resources for yourself and to deny them to the competition. The worst mistake is to pull out dedicated resources because of the success to date; this can jeopardize what you've gained so far. Instead, pour more resources into it and ensure complete success.

Milk rich markets to support your company. See to the growth and well-being of your employees; do not burn them out. Enroll the employees in the company vision and hold back from all-out effort until it is essential.

Too many companies treat employees as expendable resources, to be used up, discarded, and replaced. That attitude may yield short-term results, but it is ultimately self-destructive, because no one will want to come work for you.

When you enter a segment that is hard to sell to and that requires special support and development, the situation is difficult. Decide quickly to either get in or get out.

You should push ahead only if the return for your efforts is great, either because of immediate payoff or because the segment is vital.

Make a quick decision: stay with the segment and make it a success, or pull out of it altogether and cut your losses. If others have that responsibility, make them decide quickly to push through to success or to abandon the segment completely.

When a segment ties up significant resources for an extended period of time, allowing the competition to challenge you with fewer resources, the situation is trapped. Rethink your approach while seeking to block the competition's inroads.

Even if the eventual return from this segment is significant, the demand on resources prevents you from competing as well in other segments, and your overall return may decline.

Do you really want and need this segment? Is there some way that you can get a better return with fewer resources? Is there a more general (or more custom) approach you can take? While seeking these answers, find ways to nullify the competition's attempts to attack you.

How do you deal with a well-organized, well-financed company about to attack your market directly? Gain control of something they desire, and use it for leverage.

Face it: you'll probably lose a direct competition with them. Your solution, then, is to develop or acquire technology, products, and/or customers that they want or need and to use that as a base for negotiation.

When you have to respond quickly to the competition or lose the segment altogether, the situation is desperate. Fight back hard; let the company know how serious things are.

This is when you're on the receiving end of an ascendant situation: the competition has made serious inroads into your segment and has won key accounts.

Hang on to every customer, every account. Make it clear to your customers and to the competition that you are not giving up, and that they are going to have to devote increasing resources to that segment. Make it very clear to all the employees just how bad things are going in the market, to help unify them and to get their best effort.

Place your employees in a do-or-die situation against powerful competition, and they will move heaven and earth to accomplish what is asked of them. When all employees from the CEO downward face the same risks, then all will put forth the same effort. When faced with overwhelming odds and nowhere to go, the employees will give their all.

The key in all this: "when all employees from the CEO downward face the same risks." In an age of mobile executives and golden parachutes, it's going to take some serious commitments on the part of upper management to convince the rest of the company that risks are really shared.

In this situation, the employees do what is needed before being told, give trust and loyalty without being asked, and cooperate with one another without causing problems.

There may be some who, even under the circumstances previously described, will continue to cavil and slack. Fire them.

Stock options aren't enough to make employees remain, nor are payroll cut-off dates enough to make them give their all.

Golden handcuffs and dire threats don't always work, especially with engineers and other developers. Indeed, they may have the opposite effect, driving them away from the company.

When faced with the final do-or-die effort, employees may act upset or be stressed, but once the effort starts, they work hard, long, and without complaint.

Anticipation is worse than the fact, and once they see the shared commitment and effort, the employees settle in to the task.

It is the nature of people to defend when challenged; to strive hardest when there is no alternative; to expand when superior.

Use this nature to focus their efforts according to the various situations you face.

As CEO, you guide the company into a high-risk situation, as if crossing a river and then burning the bridge behind you. Once in that situation, you focus and release the energy of the company. You make irrevocable decisions and guide the company ahead, for there is no turning back.

In short, your responsibility is to unify the company and to lead it into areas of risk.

Both tasks are necessary. Without unity, the company will splinter under the pressure of risk; without risk, the employees will not give their best effort.

Learn to deal with the nine situations, with market expansion or contraction, and with the plans and reactions of others.

There are specific leadership challenges associated with each of the nine situations, with the state of success in the market, and with how the employees and the competition react to these conditions.

As CEO, you should be calm, confidential, even-handed and organized.

Four principles. *Calm:* you need to keep your head and wits about you. *Confidential:* you need to be able to keep a secret. *Even-handed:* you need to be fair and balanced in managing, rewarding, and disciplining others. *Organized:* you need to know what is going on and be able to convey that information to others in a timely fashion.

You should be able to deal with highly sensitive information, keeping it from employees when necessary.

Do not confuse discretion with dishonesty, though. Lying to your employees will almost always backfire in the end, corroding their trust, loyalty, and respect, as well as your own ethics.

Remain unpredictable to your competitors and keep your true intentions secret.

A general principle is that the less the competition knows about you and the less they can predict your actions, the more broadly they have to prepare or respond and the more resources and effort they consume.

Be prepared to change product specification and to alter marketing plans as required to keep the competition confused.

Be sure, however, that you don't confuse your own marketing and engineering divisions in the process.

If you don't know the plans of other companies, you cannot form appropriate strategies and alliances.

You need to know what's going on in the rest of the industry—not just among actual or potential competitors, but among all relevant companies.

If you don't understand the marketplace, you cannot create successful products.

Your product must meet the needs and/or desires of the potential customers so well that they are willing to spend their money to buy it instead of any competing product or any other use they might have for that money.

If you don't hire experienced developers and marketers, you cannot fully exploit development technologies, distribution channels, and market opportunities.

Get people who know what they're doing and who know what you want to do. If you're going to do multimedia applications, hire experienced multimedia developers, experienced multimedia product managers, experienced multimedia marketers.

A CEO who doesn't understand even one of these three principles shouldn't be running a company.

To summarize: know the competition; know the market; hire the right people.

Reward employees appropriately, regardless of company policy.

While there should be established guidelines for promotion, bonuses, profit sharing, etc., do not be limited by those guidelines. When appropriate, give rewards above and beyond the norm: cash, promotions, extra vacation, a paid trip somewhere, a custom t-shirt. Recognition for effort and accomplishments goes a long way.

Guide the company without worrying about precedence.

Too many decisions and policies are shaped by inertia and tradition. Be willing to make the right choice, regardless of how things have been done in the past.

Tell the employees what to do without divulging all your plans. Focus on the benefits and rewards; minimize company troubles.

There is a fine line here between keeping the employees focused and hiding important information from them. The guideline: if the issue is likely to be resolved without a significant impact on the employees, then you probably don't need to discuss it at large. At the same time, you need to be aware that, as mentioned before, an information vacuum will fill itself, often with rumors and ever more frantic concerns.

Finally, as said before, don't lie. Withhold information if you must, but don't lie.

Lead them into high-risk situations, and they will make it through. Present them with impossible challenges, and they will surpass them. When faced with the greatest dangers, your employees can achieve the greatest success.

When there is a true high-risk situation, use it as a rallying point for the employees. Do not underestimate what they can and will accomplish when faced with insurmountable odds. But, and this is critical, all in the company must share the risks and the efforts, as well as the rewards. Employees who think they may lose their jobs, but don't see a similar risk for you and other senior managers, will be more focused on lining up a new job in advance than in helping you succeed.

If you do this, you can manage a large company as if managing a single person.

The company will respond to direction as would an individual.

Time to market is the essence of competition.

This applies both to initial product release and to significant revisions: the product that gets there first has a major advantage over all others.

Time to market can be measured from several points: (1) when the competition learns of your development; (2) when the industry learns of your development; (3) when potential customers learn of your development; (4) when the product become relevant (and when it might become irrelevant or obsolete); (5) when customers voice their desire or demands for the product. Good security can effectively shorten time to market in the first three cases; market forces influence the fourth. The last case is the most critical situation: you risk both angering your customers and handing the competition a great opportunity to take market share from you.

When you are ready to roll out your product, tighten security and shut down communications with your competitors.

Go quiet shortly before launch; create uncertainty in the competition's mind as to what you're releasing and when.

When an opportunity appears, move rapidly to take advantage of it. Discern what the competition wants and strive to gain it first, anticipating their plans.

This is probably easier to do with equipment and hardware than with software and other forms of information and entertainment, but that makes it all the more important to be able to do this in all categories. Anticipate the competition so that you can block them from markets that you would like to capture.

When you go up against a powerful competitor, you must distract and divide the opposition. You need to make a good showing against that competitor and thus cause hesitation and doubt in those that might ally with them.

Other companies will tend to side with the firm that they think will be the eventual winner. You must sow doubts among those firms, so that they don't throw in with the competition and thus make your success even more difficult.

In this way, you can undermine potential alliances and win customers back.

Many of the "strategic alliances" of the past, especially those designed to establish "standards," have failed because competing companies offered a current desirable technology as opposed to an uncertain future technology.

The essence of competition is to observe others closely as a guide to your own actions.

Again, to ignore the competition as you push ahead is dangerous and can be fatal. You must know what they are doing and understand why they are doing it.

Your key task is to appear to accommodate the plans of your competitors.

The more you seem to play into their hands, the more unprepared they will be for your actual course of action.

With total focus on your competitors, you can render their leadership ineffective at a distance. This is the height of skill.

The idea: use a variety of methods, actions, information, and misinformation to lead the competition into decisions that benefit your company.

Again, you need to recognize the different competitive situations in which you can find yourself, and you need to respond to each appropriately, both externally and internally. You call forth the best of your employees by putting them into high-risk situations and then rewarding them, individually and collectively, when they come through.

Chapter 12

Competing by Influence

I had the most fun writing this chapter. I've been in all the roles mentioned here: early adopter, customer, reviewer, journalist, industry analyst, author, developer, marketer, and, of course, competitor. I know what has and hasn't worked in influencing me; likewise, I've had my share of successes and failures in influencing others.

I consider this one of the most important chapters in the book. Why? Because so many companies do such a poor, or at least inconsistent, job of influencing those they need to influence, whether it be customers, the press, the industry, or the competition. I have been amazed and frustrated over the years at the illogical, insufficient, and often counterproductive approaches to marketing products, image, and technology by so-called professional marketing types, or by those who think they know how to market.

Sun Tzu's twelfth chapter is on attacking with fire; it is, of course, an easy leap from lighting brushfires to issuing press releases and leaking rumors. It's interesting how many of the tactics map so well from one topic to the other.

There are five ways to compete by influence.

To influence is "to affect or alter by indirect or intangible means." To compete by influence is to use means other than standard development, marketing, and sales to gain an advantage over the competition.

First, influence the competition.

Enter into negotiations with them. Talk with their partners. Talk with their customers. Leak to them information that will make them reconsider their plans. Keep from them information that would make them reconsider their plans. Give them lots to think about, while you stay focused. Misdirect, mislead, and see if you can get them to chase their own tails.

Second, influence the press.

This does not mean to subvert journalistic integrity; that not only damages your own integrity, it almost always has negative consequences in the long run. It *does* mean to court the press, to treat writers and editors with forethought and respect, to not underestimate or insult their intelligence, to make yourself and other key employees available for interviews and questions, and to provide them with review products and lots of useful, interesting, and accurate information. This last point is especially important, because most writers and all editors will smell hype and puffery a mile away and will almost always react unfavorably to it.

Third, influence the industry.

Produce products with ideas worthy of imitation; that casts you into the role of a standard setter, and makes others take you more seriously. Network with key people in other companies. Establish a strong presence at industry conferences and seminars, raising your visibility. Have your employees publish papers and appear on panels.

In all these efforts, you seek to influence not just the management of other companies, but their employees also, as well as investors and industry analysts.

Fourth, influence customers.

Influencing customers requires several interlocking steps. Let the customer know that your product exists and that it meets some key requirements or desires they have. Convince the customer that your product will be worth the investment (money, time, effort, mind-share, training, support) they will make in it. Persuade the customer to decide to make that investment now (or at least by a certain date) rather than sometime in the future. Create a corporate image that makes the customer desire to associate with you and your products.

Advertising is part of this, as is press coverage, word of mouth, and (when appropriate) direct customer contact. Think of new ways to influence, but beware of clumsy manipulation: customers will detect it and will get upset with you.

Fifth, influence technology.

Introduce technology that leads others to adopt, build upon, conform to, or coordinate with your technology. This increases the value and desirability of your technology in the eyes of customers, which in turn leads even more firms to adopt, etc., your technology. Successful examples of this include the Intel x86 processors and Microsoft Windows.

Be warned that you can influence technology without succeeding at it yourself. Xerox PARC developed many key aspects of the graphical user interface (GUI), but had no commercial success with it. Apple, with the Macintosh, achieved commercial success for GUIs, but ultimately paved the way for Microsoft to dominate the market.

To use influence, circumstances must be appropriate, and the right means and contacts are required.

Poorly timed or poorly conceived influence is worse than no influence at all, since it can cause a negative backlash.

There are key periods during the year to use influence.

This depends in part on both your product and your audience, particularly if the market is institutional (government, educational, corporate) and has key budgeting and purchasing times during the year. It can also depend upon lead times in publications for editorial material and advertisements. Finally, you may want to coordinate your efforts with key trade shows or other conferences related to your products, technology, or industry.

Use influence when concerns over related issues are rising.

If you're too early, no one will care or notice. If interest has already peaked, you'll be seen as someone else trying to jump on the bandwagon.

In using influence, there are situations that you must be aware of and handle appropriately. If influence is having effect within the competition, match it with efforts outside that company.

When you see the competition reacting to your efforts to influence them, you can multiply the effect by influencing other areas (the press, the industry, customers, technology) at the same time.

However, if the management and employees of that company are handling things well, then stand back and wait.

Don't spend time, effort, and capital on an effort that will have little effect.

When the influence has run its course, then press your advantage if it will be to your benefit; otherwise, hold off.

Sometimes it's good to follow up the influence with market and product actions; sometimes it's best to appear aloof and independent.

If you can influence factors outside of the competing firms, then don't wait for an opportunity to influence matters inside those firms, but push ahead. Be sure, however, to always wait for an appropriate time.

You may be laying the groundwork for having influence inside the competition by influencing factors outside of it.

Be sure you are in the proper position to benefit from your efforts.

Be prepared to follow up or act upon the results of your attempts to use influence.

Take care, lest your efforts backfire.

For example, if you manage to create significant interest in your product and/or technology, but then can't deploy it quickly, you may lose influence and credibility and damage your reputation.

Your attempts at influence may spread quickly at first, but they will die down sooner or later.

Face it: people and institutions have short attention spans. This is why you need to be ready to take advantage of influence even as you wield it.

Your employees must be aware of these means of competing by influence and must be prepared to deal with them.

Remember, all these efforts can be directed against you as well. Make sure you and your employees are sensitive to efforts by others to influence your company.

Those who use influence to aid in competition show intelligence; those who use technology show strength. Technology can block a competitor's advances, but will not affect their resources.

We often think that the best technology, the best product will win. History teaches otherwise. Many excellent products have died prematurely because the company could not exert the necessary influence, while less-than-excellent products have survived or even thrived because their company could.

It is a waste of time and effort to gain market share or to win customers, and then to fail to take full and timely advantage of it or to not reward those who made it possible.

Two separate failings: to not press your advantage, and to not reward those who got you there in the first place. Either failing will undermine what success you have achieved.

A wise board of directors considers the company's plans and policies carefully, and a skilled CEO carries them out well.

The board's role is to advise, to check, and to hold the CEO accountable. The CEO's role is to lead, to direct, and to implement.

Don't follow a given course of action unless it will benefit the company.

This may seem utterly obvious, but many companies end up on paths that at best represent a holding pattern and, at worst, a downward spiral.

Don't assign personnel to a product unless it can succeed.

Obvious, yet often ignored. There are lots of reasons why people are assigned to products that are unlikely to succeed: turf wars, wishful thinking, internal politics, empire-building, and external image.

Don't compete with another firm unless it is critical to do so.

Unnecessary competition wastes vital resources and lessens the chances of success and profit.

Directors shouldn't dictate a course of action out of pique, nor should a CEO attack another company out of resentment. Anger and resentment pass, but failed companies are seldom restored and lost employees seldom regained.

How many companies have been damaged or destroyed because of the pride and ego of the CEO? Yet it is not the CEO but the employees who usually suffer.

A wise board is thoughtful, and a skilled CEO is careful. The company is kept whole, and the jobs of its employees are preserved.

In short, make sure you don't cause layoffs because of poor judgment based on an emotional response to the competition.

Influence and fire have much in common indeed, including this caution: think carefully about what you are doing lest you get burned yourself in the process.

Chapter 13

Gathering Intelligence

We live, as we have been told for years, in the Information Age. Data floods us from all sides, and our challenge is to extract useful intelligence from it; after all, it's easier to find gold nuggets in a mountain stream than in the Mississippi.

Sun Tzu, in his final chapter, talks about the need to gather intelligence about the enemy. With great passion, he points out that, given the terrible costs of war, to remain uninformed of the enemy's situation out of an unwillingness to spend a little money or to grant honors is inhumane. How true.

When a company, division, or development team is formed and started on a significant development project, the costs will average $100,000 per year per person for salary, benefits, administrative support, office space, equipment, and other expenditures.

There will be great stress both at work and at home for the employees, they will be exhausted from working long hours, and the lives of their families will be disrupted as well.

Development may go on for months or years in order to release a single product and win out over competing firms.

In short, there are tremendous personal and resource costs in bringing a new product to market.

Given the great costs and sacrifices involved, for a CEO and others to remain less than fully informed on the marketplace, on the industry, on technology and tools, and on the competition because of reluctance to spend a few thousand dollars per year on information sources is inhumane. Such a CEO has failed the employees, the board of directors, and the company itself.

Besides being inhumane, it's also downright stupid. It just makes no sense to spend vast amounts of money, usually millions of dollars, and vast amounts of employees' time (and lives) to bring a product to market, and then to jeopardize it all because of an unwillingness to spend a tiny fraction of those resources to gather intelligence.

Good industry intelligence enables a wise board and a skilled CEO to win out over competitors and to have spectacular results.

It's not enough to be wise and skilled, you must also be informed.

This kind of intelligence does not come from wishful thinking, nor from history, nor from spreadsheets. It comes only from current sources of information.

Too many products, too many business plans are based on hope, old markets, and the 5% fallacy ("If we capture just five percent of the market...").

There are five major types of intelligence: industry sources; inside contacts; competition sources; disinformation; and field research.

Note that "intelligence" includes disseminating information as well as collecting it.

When all five sources of intelligence are used, the whole is greater than the sum of the parts, and it is of immense value to you.

The interaction and cross-checking among the sources helps to sort out what's important and what's real.

Industry sources are periodicals, journals, newsletters, electronic information services, the Internet/Web, consultants, and contacts within other companies.

These are sources available to anyone who wants to spend the money, time, and other resources required to glean information from them.

Inside contacts are private sources of information within other firms, particularly the competition.

These are personal contacts, people within other firms who are willing to talk about what they know. The most valuable contacts—and the hardest to come by—are those inside the firms with which you directly compete. The next most valuable are those who have contacts inside or dealings with competing firms, and so on. Each step in the chain between you and the competition introduces noise and error, so you want that chain to be as short as possible. Lacking that, you can use multiple sources to help cross-check one another.

Competition sources are products, manuals, literature, seminars, advertising, and other sources offered publicly by the competition.

The best information about the competition (other than from inside contacts) comes directly from the competition's own materials. Read their ads and press releases. Attend trade shows where their executives are speaking. Buy their products and study them, including the documentation. Call up tech support. Get all the sales materials they offer publicly. Attend seminars they put on. Spend time in their on-line service conferences. Become a certified developer.

Disinformation is erroneous information about your company, plans, and products leaked to the competition.

Nature abhors a vacuum, and that's as true in the virtual world as in the real world. Lack of information about your plans and efforts calls attention to itself and increases the competition's efforts (and ability) to find out what's going on. It is not enough to withhold information; something must be given in its place.

The challenge: maintaining good relations with your customers and the press while using disinformation. You want the competition to underestimate you, yet you want the press and your customers to be excited by you. It's all a matter of timing and intelligence.

Field research is visiting customers, attending seminars, taking classes, and then reporting back with the information.

Not all information will come into your company; some of the most important information has to be gathered outside. Nothing is as valuable as visiting customers on-site and seeing what the needs and concerns of the actual users are. Seminars convey far more information than can be gathered by the printed proceedings, both from direct observation of the speakers and from interaction with other participants. Likewise, ongoing education of your employees (and yourself!) brings in far more information than the mere reading of books.

Debriefing is a critical part of field research. Emphasis should be placed on the intangibles that don't appear on paper.

Therefore, you should work closest with those who are able to gather intelligence. Support and reward them generously, and be sure the information gathered remains within your company.

Too often, it is the CEO who questions the time and expense of gathering intelligence. Instead, the CEO should encourage it, demand it, and reward it.

The information gathered can only be effectively used in combination with wisdom, insight, humanity, and even-handedness.

In other words, intelligence in and of itself has little practical worth. Only when it is used appropriately can it benefit the company, its employees, its investors, and its customers.

Verifying information, especially from contacts in other companies, requires subtlety, cleverness, and delicacy.

Clumsiness can embarrass or even endanger the jobs of those sources.

If there are unplanned and unwanted leaks within your own company, confront and, if necessary, dismiss the employee.

Given that inside information is the most valuable type of intelligence, you must guard against unwanted inside information getting out. This means building a culture of internal confidence—which means being willing to trust employees with valuable information as it comes in.

Whether your aim is to broadly engage a company in competition, to capture a given market, or to win over a particular customer, you must first identify and learn about the competition's people: the executives, the marketers, the developers, the sales force. Use your sources to find this out.

The better you understand the competition's people, the better you can interpret their public statements; the better you can evaluate confidential sources; the better you can predict their behavior and performance; and the better you can mislead and manipulate them.

Take every opportunity to study and learn from competition sources. These will help you to identify relevant industry sources. They will allow you to find inside contacts. They will guide you in transmitting disinformation. And they will aid you in conducting appropriate field research.

Most companies reveal a tremendous amount about themselves in what they release publicly. Take advantage of these sources to build up your other sources.

You must be steeped in all five sources of intelligence; these are guided by competition sources, so time, money, and effort must be devoted to obtaining and understanding that type of intelligence.

In other words, first spend money on the competition's products, gather the competition's literature, read the competition's press releases.

If you're smart, you'll assign your best people to gathering intelligence. This information is essential for competition, and all the company's employees rely upon it for their decisions.

There are individuals who are very good at dealing with each of the types of information sources. Find them, use them.

It is, of course, ironic that companies deeply rooted in an information-based economy often make such poor use of the information sources available to them. It is as if steel producers made no use of high-quality steel for tools and mills. But such firms are likely to be supplanted by those that indeed know how to effectively filter and use the torrent of data. Think of it as evolution in action.

Afterword

This book grew out of an incident in the early days of Pages Software Inc. During an engineering meeting, Bruce Henderson—who had spent several years in the US Marine Corps—quoted a maxim from *Suntzu pingfa* (Sun Tzu's *The Art of War*), a book with which I had been familiar for years and which I had quoted at Pages from time to time. This set me to thinking about how applicable Sun Tzu was to competing in the technology and information industries. I went through the first chapter of *Suntzu pingfa* and started rephrasing Sun Tzu's maxims to that end. Before I had finished, I was convinced that there was something of real worth there, and I decided to press on and do all of *Suntzu pingfa*, thinking that the result might be of worth to others in the industry.

What I didn't expect was that it would be more than three years before I finished the book. It wasn't the writing *per se* that took so long; it was that my time was consumed by work at Pages—a start-up software venture—and what spare time I had went to my family. I think the book is much better for the time it took. The ideas inside have been able to stew and simmer for a few years, during which I was up to my eyeballs in the topics to be addressed.

The technique of producing this book was straightforward, though not easy. I worked with several different English translations of *Suntzu pingfa*. I would study a given maxim in all the versions simultaneously, determine what the essential concept was, then use that as the basis for a parallel maxim appropriate to the topic at hand. Of course, not all the translators agreed in their interpretation of a given maxim; sometimes they differed radically. In those cases, I was guided by the essential concept and how well it fit into the appropriate contemporary situation. Likewise, there were disagreements among the translators as to the ordering of some maxims, and some did rearranging to clarify the structure and to reduce unnecessary redundancy.

While I did drop or move the occasional maxim, the maxims in each chapter of *The Art of Ware* generally match in order and concept those found in *Suntzu pingfa*. The biggest exception: Chapter 11, where I did wholesale rearranging of maxims to produce a more coherent (and less redundant) presentation. You might find it interesting to compare my order with that found in a more traditional translation of *Suntzu pingfa*.

I find myself wishing that I knew five, ten, fifteen years ago what I understand now about product development and running a company. But that's the eternal cycle: good judgment comes from experience, and experience comes from poor judgment. On the other hand, if I get involved with yet another start-up, I'll certainly be better prepared.

I hope you've enjoyed the book and that it's helped you towards more success, however you might define that. If you've got comments, criticisms, or other feedback, please drop me a line; details are in the next section ("An Invitation"). In the meantime, take care, and I'll see you on the bitstream.

An Invitation

In *Suntzu pingfa*, Sun Tzu only wrote the maxims. Commentary was added through the centuries by other military leaders, philosophers, and writers. They interpreted and expanded upon his thoughts, often providing military anecdotes to support a particular concept.

I would like *The Art of 'Ware* to grow into a compilation of insight, observations, and wisdom from the industry itself. To that end, I am soliciting commentary for all the maxims in this book. Should a sufficient number of acceptable commentaries be submitted, they will be incorporated into subsequent editions of *The Art of 'Ware*, adding to or replacing the ones I have already written. Much as in with editions of *Suntzu pingfa*, each commentary will be individually credited (in other words, your name will be right there in each commentary printed), and there can be multiple commentaries on a single maxim.

Here's the fine print, right up front. First, acceptance and inclusion (or exclusion) of a given commentary is entirely at the discretion and whim of myself and the publishers. Second, you won't get paid anything. Third, you'll assign all rights (on a nonexclusive basis) to the publisher. Fourth, you'll have to sign and return a form agreeing to all this.

For more information, or to give me any feedback about the book you might have, contact me at the following addresses:

e-mail:	bwebster@bix.com
p-mail:	*Art of 'Ware* Commentary, P.O. Box 500750, San Diego, CA, 92150-0750
vox:	619/672-4542

Bibliography

Suntzu pingfa

There are a surprising number of English translations of *Suntzu pingfa*, and new ones appear on a regular basis. Here are several currently in print, with my comments and observations about each. They are listed alphabetically by translator/editor. Many (as noted) include traditional commentary by Chinese generals and philosophers during the centuries following Sun Tzu.

Ames, Roger. *Sun Tzu: The Art of Warfare*. Ballantine Books, New York, 1993. Based on a 2100-year-old copy of Sun Tzu's text found in a tomb near Linyi in 1972. Contains extensive discussion (about 100 pages) of history, background, and philosophy. The *Suntzu pingfa* section has both Chinese and English text, though no commentary. Also has additional Sun Tzu texts and references found in Linyi site. Has an extensive bibliography.

Clavell, James. *The Art of War*. Dell Publishing, New York, 1988. This uses the Lionel Giles translation (first published in 1910) and has only a little traditional commentary, plus a brief introduction by Clavell.

159

Cleary, Thomas. *The Art of War*. Shambhala, Boston, 1988. Contains a 40-page introduction by Cleary. Has traditional commentary interspersed with Sun Tzu's maxims. Also available in a pocket-sized version without introduction or commentary.

Griffith, Samuel B. *The Art of War*. Oxford University Press, Oxford, 1971. Probably the best-known English translation; has traditional commentary, as well as significant background material.

Hanzhang, Tao. *Sun Tzu's Art of War: The Modern Chinese Interpretation*. (Translated by Yuan Shibing.) Sterling Publishing Co., Inc., New York, 1990. This is an English translation of an analysis of *Suntzu pingfa* by General Hanzhang, a senior officer in the People's Liberation Army in China. He analyzes Sun Tzu's maxims as they apply to actual military issues, drawing upon various examples in Chinese military history. The actual English text of *Suntzu pingfa* is given in an appendix and is identical to Griffith's, though it has no commentary.

Huang, J. H. *Sun Tzu: The New Translation*. William Morrow and Company, Inc., New York, 1993. Also based on 2100-year-old Linyi texts. Has extensive analysis (in parallel columns) of the text itself, though no traditional commentary. It also has a parallel set of chapters offering discussion of the author's translation. An extensive set of appendices includes five previously unknown Sun Tzu-related texts found in the Linyi documents. Competes with Sawyer (below) as the most scholarly and exhaustive presentation and analysis, yet readable. Huang's translation often differs quite significantly from more traditional translations; he offers detailed and fascinating support for his interpretations.

Sawyer, Ralph D. *Sun-tzu: The Art of War*. Westview Press, Boulder, CO, 1994. An excellent all-around treatment. Sawyer spends 170 pages setting the background of Chinese military history of the era in question, gives his own translation (with no commentaries) of *Suntzu pingfa* and some of the Sun Tzu-related Linyi documents, then has another 100 pages of notes supporting his translation.

Tsai, Chih Chung. *Sunzi Speaks: The Art of War*. (Translated by Brian Bruya.) Anchor Books, New York, 1994. A "comic strip" version of *Suntzu pingfa*, originally published in Chinese in Taiwan and then translated into English by Brian Bruya. Don't let the cartoons fool you; this is an excellent and very accessible exposition of Sun Tzu's concepts.

Wing, R. L. *The Art of Strategy*. Doubleday, New York, 1988. Has complete Chinese ideographic text with English translation on facing pages. The translator attempts to make the English phrasing and word patterns match the Chinese, and to give the text a more general application to life; the result is very lyrical and accessible. No traditional commentary. Set up as a personal workbook for dealing with conflict, with each chapter divided into four sections, yielding 52 weekly readings.

Other Books

An exhaustive list would also be exhausting, so I've limited it to those books that have had an impact on me for one reason or another, and that I think are relevant to the subject. Take careful notes as you go through these books; there's usually more than you'll be able to remember, and there's a lot you'll want to remember.

Brooks, Frederick P. *The Mythical Man-Month*. Addison-Wesley, Reading, MA, 1995. The *sine qua non* of software engineering and project management, updated and extended by Brooks. Every person involved in technology development, from developers to CEOs, should read this book and believe what it has to say, because it's true, whether you want it to be or not.

Covey, Stephen R. *Principle-Centered Leadership*. Summit Books, New York, 1990. A lot of folks don't like Covey, mostly because he makes them uncomfortable with his talk of ethics, integrity, and principles. That's exactly why they should read him.

Davidow, William H. *Marketing High Technology*. The Free Press, New York, 1986. The first chapter is entitled "Crush the Competition", which pretty much sets the tone for the book. Davidow's background is in marketing semiconductor technology, which is a refreshing change from all the software-oriented books in this list.

Davis, Alan M. *201 Principles of Software Development*. McGraw-Hill, Inc., New York, 1995. The title says it all: 201 principles, each on a separate page with a brief explanation and a reference. A book to keep handy and browse often.

De Marco, Tom, and Lister, Timothy. *Peopleware*. Dorset House Publishing Co., New York, 1987. An excellent book on the details of setting up and running an effective technology development group. As with *The Mythical Man-Month*, you ignore this book at your own peril.

Kelly, Kevin. *Out of Control*. Addison-Wesley, Reading, MA, 1994. Kelly, the executive editor of *WIRED*, captures and well articulates the cross-fertilization and convergence of biological and mechanical architectures in technology, economics, politics, and society at large. I find this book both disturbing and exhilarating, which is probably the proper response.

Keyes, Jessica (editor). *Software Engineering Productivity Handbook*. Windcrest/McGraw-Hill, New York, 1993. If Brooks' thin volume establishes the framework, this thick one (37 contributors, 69 short chapters) fills in lots and lots of details. The first chapter alone, Keyes' survey of the field, would make the book worthwhile for most development groups, but there is so much more.

Moore, Geoffrey. *Crossing the Chasm*. Harper Collins, New York, 1991. The thesis is obvious when you examine it, yet many technology companies have failed to heed it and have fallen headfirst into the chasm, or are in the process of doing so. Read the book to learn more.

Peters, Tom. *Liberation Management*. Fawcett Columbine, New York, 1992. This book is thick, a bit scattered, and not easy to get through. But it should still be on your reading list.

Strassman, Paul A. *The Business Value of Computers: An Executive's Guide.* The Information Economics Press, New Canaan, CT, 1992. His thesis, backed up with exhaustive statistics: there is no relationship in American industry between spending for computers and any resulting profits and productivity. Read this book to guide you in product development and marketing.

Webster, Bruce F. *Pitfalls of Object-Oriented Development.* M&T Books, New York, 1995. While this book was written to address object-oriented development, many of the pitfalls described apply to software and technology development in general.

Yourdon, Edward. *Decline & Fall of the American Programmer.* Yourdon Press, Englewood Cliffs, NJ, 1992. A provocative work on why American programmers are (or appear to be) fat, lazy, overpaid, and underproductive. Well worth reading; don't miss the appendix on "The Programmer's Bookshelf."

Index